THIS RE-INVENT 360° JOURNAL BELONGS TO:

_____

_____

_____

_____

START DATE: _____   FINISH DATE: _____

For information about permission to reproduce selections from this book, email shaz@reinvent360journal.com.

Visit my website at ReInvent360Journal.com

PUBLISHER'S DISCLAIMER

While the publisher and author have used their best efforts in preparing this book, they make no guarantees with regards to individual results. The advice and strategies contained herein are designed to motivate the user towards reaching a desired outcome.

ISBN 978-0-578-42405-7

Written & Created by Shaz Alidina
Co-Written, Designed & Edited by Chris Jones

FIRST EDITION

PRAISE FOR
RE-INVENT 360° JOURNAL

"Re-Invent 360° Journal is deceptive: what appears to be a simple set of exercises in fact gets right to the core of how ordinary people (like all of us) cannot only accomplish extraordinary things, but also 'live your best life.' It resonates very nicely with a lot of what I learned at Harvard Business School and with my 30 years of working in Hollywood."

Mark Gill
President & CEO, Solstice Studios

"With all the distractions in life, one tends to loose focus and passion. Re-Invent 360° Journal will help you achieve your life goals by staying persistent on whats really important to achieve greatness! This book can change your life! Very well done, Shaz Alidina!"

Muhammed Owais Pardesi
CEO of Cosmos Group (Tanzania).

"I've been an avid journal user for many years, and have seen my share of different ones since I first became a coach. I LOVE what this journal does — it's got all the things needed to keep you on track with an easy-to-follow flow and great design. I highly recommend it!"

Marc Mawhinney
Business Coach, Natural Born Coaches

"The Re-Invent 360° Journal is a powerful tool of transformation for all those who seek more clarity and intention in their lives."

Sahara Rose
*#1 Internationally Bestselling Author of Idiots Guide to Ayurveda.
Founder of Eat Feel Fresh, Host of Highest Self Podcast and Mind-Body*

PRAISE FOR
RE-INVENT 360° JOURNAL

"Don't set another goal before trying the Re-Invent 360° Journal. This book takes you beyond your goals setting! It will show you how to find your purpose first then create success around it. It carries the top secrets toward achieving an extraordinary quality of life and the pillars of self-mastery. When you figure that out, that's when you start to taste the kind of success that this journal can create for you.

Damien O'Donohoe,
CEO of IKON Media and Entertainment
Owner of Caribbean Premier League & G-Finity Elites Series Australia.

"The Re-Invent 360° Journal was great at helping me get clear on what I need to be focusing on. I like the steps I went through in preparation for using the journal. I believe that was the most important feature in making the journal more effective in getting the results any user would be looking for."

Jaynee Sasso
CEO of Brisance Coaching & Consulting

"Everyone faces challenges and difficulties, and these are intrinsic part of life. Yet it seems that some people have full control over their hardships. What do they do differently? This Journal has showed me that the magic lies in how one decides to focus their time and energy. By providing an easy to follow routine to manage your day to day life, you too can become a high achiever!"

Danish Dhaman
CEO of Ora

CONTENTS

THANK YOU!

I am excited that you are taking the first step on the journey of achieving your dreams by recreating yourself from the inside out. Your Re-Invent 360° Journal is just one resource in helping you to achieve your dreams through specific and meaningful daily actions and habits.

Your Re-Invent 360° Journal is designed to help you to purposefully begin each day, construct empowering morning routines that inspire you to action, and remind you to express gratitude for what you have and will receive as you pursue your passion while looking inward to consider what you can improve upon for the next day. These five key elements—goals, habits, actions, gratitude, and reflection—are instrumental in creating your best life and your Re-Invent 360° Journal will be your guide.

I hope that as you embrace this journal and take it wherever you go, that you open it up throughout the day to review your goals and keep them in the front of your mind.

Please stay connected to the Re-Invent 360° Community where you can share your journey, get inspired, ask questions, and know that others around the world are using this same journal that you hold to pursue their best life.

Live Inspired.

Shaz Alidina

RE-INVENT 360° JOURNAL

I created the Re-Invent 360° Journal to give you the guidance and inspiration you need to simplify your daily process to only those things that have a direct impact in living your best and most successful life.

Having worked with high achievers across the world in many industries, the one commodity they all agree upon that leads to success is where they focus their time and energy. The Re-Invent 360° Journal takes the guesswork out of where to focus you best energy and gives you a daily blueprint for creating lasting habits leading to success and fulfillment.

As a member of the Re-Invent 360° Journal community, you'll have access to these great perks:

- Daily accountability
- A community of high achievers like yourself
- Exclusive content only found within the group

JOIN THE RE-INVENT 360° COMMUNITY
(IT'S FREE!)

www.ReInvent360Journal.com/community

> **BELIEVE SO DEEPLY**
>
> **THAT YOU NO LONGER**
>
> **QUESTION THAT**
>
> **IT'S POSSIBLE**

JUSTIN PERRY

SETTING YOUR
INTENTION

WHAT DO I REALLY WANT? BE SPECIFIC.

Take a few minutes or more to think about what it is that you want to become in the next 100 days. Think of your starting point and what you will need to do to get there. An old saying worth repeating is that you have to "be specific to be terrific." That means you have to say exactly what it is that you want to be. It's not enough to say, "I want to be a personal trainer at a gym." You should dig deeper and be more specific and say, "I want to be a celebrity weight loss coach," if that truly is your goal. Your mind is like a computer. Whatever you ask it will find a way to get you the information or answers that you seek. So the more specific you make your request, the more likely that you're going to get back what you ask of it. Use the space below to write your initial thoughts.

_____

_____

_____

_____

_____

_____

_____

_____

_____

_____

_____

_____

_____

_____

_____

_____

_____

_____

_____

_____

_____

WHAT'S MY PURPOSE?

People keep asking themselves...what is my life purpose? There are shelves of books about it, YouTube videos on it, and articles discussing it. To find your purpose, do a little soul searching on a sheet of paper. Answer these questions to get your mind going:

What do you love? (e.g. Tiger Woods loves to play golf. Tony Robbins loves to transform people's lives.)

_____

_____

_____

_____

What do you notice? What grabs your attention? (e.g. A hairstylist notices when someone's hair is out of place. An auto detailer notices dirty cars.)

_____

_____

_____

_____

What do you love to talk about? (e.g. Darren Rowse loves to talk about blogging. Amy Porterfield loves to talk about online marketing.)

_____

_____

_____

_____

What would you do for free? (e.g. Giving service to the poor and needy.)

_____

_____

_____

_____

What do you love to learn about? Is there a common thread? (e.g. sports, fashion, etc)

_____

_____

_____

_____

What sparks your creativity? (e.g. Explore the unknown. Writing in a journal.)

_____

_____

_____

_____

What problem do you want to solve? (e.g. Bill Gates wanted everyone to have a personal computer at home. David William of Make-a-Wish Foundation wanted to fulfill a "wish" for children with life-threatening medical conditions.)

_____

_____

_____

_____

What makes you happy? (e.g. Writing, sports, cooking, building, designing, coaching, helping people succeed)

_____

_____

_____

_____

What are your talents and strengths? (e.g. Singing, playing guitar, drawing, inspiring people, creative direction, researching, serving people)

_____

_____

_____

_____

What are your skills and expertise? (e.g. video production, web design, project management, corporate training, technical writing, copywriting, programming)

_____   _____

_____   _____

_____   _____

As you perform this exercise, you'll begin to see a pattern emerge. You can even ask trusted friends or people on your favorite social media networks what they think your talents are, what you're good at, or what your expertise is. Sometimes others see what we become blind to seeing.

DREAM BIG, ACT BIGGER!

The thought must be followed by immediate action. If not, fear sets into your mind and you begin to think your way out of your purpose. One of the worst things that can happen to you is to think about something big, see and feel yourself in that beautiful situation, and then not take any action. You tell yourself, "Someday" and that day never comes. Another scenario is that you feel "Imposter's Syndrome," the belief that you aren't qualified enough to be called an expert. The truth is this: if you know more than your audience, you are the expert in the room. So be confident!

Let's take action now. On a separate piece of paper, write down a purpose statement and give yourself a powerful name (e.g. The Weight Loss Guru or The King of Fitness) and add some images and quotes. Put it somewhere visible to you. Then begin to jot down a list of the experts in your niche and seek them out in books, online articles, magazine stories, and YouTube videos. Learn what they have learned. Follow in their footsteps. Immerse yourself in becoming.

Keep in mind that if you don't direct your steps towards what you really want now, one day you will realize that you are further from it than you were before. Remember: "The best time to plant a tree was 10 years ago, but the second best time is NOW." Keep a copy of your purpose statement in the blank space below.

My Purpose Statement

_____

_____

DEFINING YOUR VALUES

Values highlight what we stand for and guide our behaviour, providing us with a personal code of conduct that drives our purpose. When we honor our core values consistently, we experience fulfillment and the euphoria of living according to the purpose that we have set for ourselves. When we don't, we are incongruent and more likely to escape into habits that don't serve our purpose or us.

How to define your values:

Take a deep breath and empty your mind. (This will help you centre yourself and help you get into the right mental and emotional state.)

Make a list of your current values (e.g. health, family, education). Possible values to consider:

- Passion
- Love
- Freedom
- Growth
- Health
- Creativity
- Achievement
- Contribution
- Happiness
- Connection

Ask: What do I value most, and in which order do my values need to be in to achieve the destiny I desire and deserve?

Group these values under related themes (e.g. Love, connection, passion)

Select one value from the group that best represents the group. (e.g. Love)

See which values you might want to get rid of and which you might add in order to create the quality of life you truly want.

- **Column 1:** Write them down your ranked value
- **Column 2:** How well you are honouring each value by scoring each on a scale of 0 to 10, where 10 represents optimally living the value
- **Column 3:** Write your action plan describing your action steps to increase the score.

Repeat this exercise each month to assess your progress. This determines what's really important and meaningful to YOU. See the chart below.

Value	Rate	Action to Take
Mindfulness & Focus	5	Practise conscious breathing
Learning & Growing	7	Read 2 books each month
Fitness & Health	6	Walk 10,000 daily

YOUR TURN

Fill out the chart below with your value, rating, and action.

Value	Rate	Action to Take

FINDING YOUR BIG WHY

Too often, we focus on the "what." What we want to be, what we want to do, or what we want to have. Today, I challenge you to ask yourself, "What is my WHY?" Discover the reason behind why you want something first. Give yourself more than twenty reasons why you want to achieve that which you want to achieve...be specific. Let that become your burning desire. Then you can allow it to lead you to the how and the what, and you'll open a world of possibilities.

Consider all of the jobs you have had, the career you have pursued, or the interests that you lean toward. Is there a common thread? Is there something about those jobs or within your career that you've been willing to deal with less than ideal standards because of something you loved? Maybe it was personnel management, to which your why may be coaching. Perhaps it was project management, to which your why may be corporate training. Take a moment to think and find the common denominator and in doing so discover your big why.

Once you have your why, you'll be ready to enter this journal and it's commitment with complete confidence.

My Big Why

_____

_____

_____

> **WE EXPAND**
>
> **WHAT WE**
>
> **FOCUS ON**

DR. WAYNE DYER

USING YOUR
JOURNAL

DAY 1

> ❝ Success is not the key to happiness. Happiness is the key to success. If you love what you are doing, you will be successful." – Herman Cain

■ THE BIG GOAL

WHAT WILL YOU ACHIEVE TODAY TO GET YOU ONE STEP CLOSER TO ACHIEVING YOUR DREAM?

I want to get my website done. I have the theme and the content

ready. Should take me 5 hours to do.

■ TAKING ACTION

WHAT STEPS WILL YOU TAKE TODAY TO ENSURE THAT YOU REACH YOUR BIG GOAL?

1 I need to install my theme.

2 I need to choose some good stock photos.

3 I need to drop in my copy and create my contact forms.

■ MORNING RITUAL

SUCCESS STARTS IN THE HABITS YOU CREATE FROM THE TIME YOU WAKE UP. HOW WILL YOU PREPARE YOUR MIND FOR ACTION TODAY?

I WILL read my 5 affirmations three times today.

I WILL watch a motivational video online.

I WILL write 3 pages in my journal to clear my mind for action.

■ GRATITUDE

PEOPLE WHO PRACTICE THE HABIT OF GRATITUDE ATTRACT MORE SUCCESS. WHO OR WHAT ARE YOU GRATEFUL FOR TODAY?

My health	Getting to play golf today
Getting to watch the sun rise	Having coffee w/ Jill later
Fresh veggies from my garden	3 new clients from yesterday

{ WE START EVERY DAY OFF WITH A QUOTE TO GET YOU
INSPIRED TO LIVE YOUR DAY WITH PASSION.

{ YOUR BIG GOAL SHOULD BE THAT ONE BURNING TASK THAT
WILL GET YOU THAT MUCH CLOSER TODAY TO ACHIEVING
YOUR DREAMS.

{ THESE ARE THE STEPS THAT ACCOMPANY THE BIG GOAL.
WHAT DO YOU HAVE TO DO TO MAKE SURE THAT YOU HIT
THE BIG GOAL TODAY?

{ WHAT THREE ACTIVITIES DO YOU NEED TO ENGAGE IN WHEN
YOUR FEET HIT THE FLOOR TO INCREASE YOUR CHANCES OF
SUCCESS TODAY?

{ WHAT OUTCOMES IN REACHING YOUR GOAL CAN YOU BE
GRATEFUL FOR NOW, EVEN THOUGH THEY HAVE NOT YET
HAPPENED? ATTRACT GOODNESS!

BE SURE TO SHARE YOUR DAILY BIG GOAL OR SOME ASPECT OF YOUR JOURNEY EACH DAY WITH OUR THRIVING FACEBOOK COMMUNITY.

PHYSICAL ACTIVITY IS KNOWN TO BOOST MOOD, ENERGY, & PRODUCTIVITY. WHAT ACTIVITY CAN YOU PERFORM TO JUMP-START YOUR DAY?

THEY SAY THAT YOUR NET WORTH IS IN YOUR NETWORK. WHO DO YOU NEED TO CONNECT WITH TODAY TO HELP YOU ACCOMPLISH YOUR BIG GOAL?

THIS IS YOUR REPORT CARD. BE HONEST. DID YOU HIT THE GOAL. IF SO, HOW DID THAT FEEL? IF NOT, WHY NOT?

THIS IS WHERE YOU BEGIN REFLECT ON HOW TO GROW FROM WHAT YOU FACED TODAY TO BE BETTER TOMORROW. WRITE AND THEN SLEEP ON IT.

DAY __1__

FACEBOOK CHECK-IN
COMMENT ON TODAY'S POST IN THE **RE-INVENT 360 JOURNAL COMMUNITY** FACEBOOK GROUP.

■ FITNESS FOCUS
A HEALTHY MIND IN A HEALTHY BODY. WHAT WILL YOU DO TODAY TO STAY ACTIVE?

I will swim 800 m in the pool after I journal.

■ CONNECTING
WHO WILL YOU TALK TO TODAY TO GET YOU ONE STEP CLOSER TOWARDS REACHING YOUR GOAL?

I'll work with John from Website Design Solutions to install my new theme.

I'll email Jill from Photos by Jill to set up a time for new headshots for my site.

(EVENING REFLECTION

■ TODAY'S WINS
NOW THAT THE DAY IS OVER, REFLECT ON WHAT YOU DID TODAY THAT HELPED YOU TO GET CLOSER TO YOUR BIG GOAL

I got the website theme in place	Got my content into my website
Scheduled headshots	Worked on basic keywording

■ PUSHING BEYOND
WHAT CAN YOU DO TOMORRROW TO IMPROVE ON THE LESSONS THAT YOU LEARNED TODAY?

I need to work on making decisions faster. I spent a lot of time on things that I shouldn't have and I over thought easy decisions. I have to be aware of analysis paralysis. I didn't need to spend three hours looking for the perfect photos.

LET THE BEAUTY

OF WHAT YOU LOVE

BE WHAT YOU DO

RUMI

START YOUR
JOURNEY

DAY ____

" *When people are determined they can overcome anything. — Nelson Mandela*

■ THE BIG GOAL

WHAT WILL YOU ACHIEVE TODAY TO GET YOU ONE STEP CLOSER TO ACHIEVING YOUR DREAM?

_____

_____

■ TAKING ACTION

WHAT STEPS WILL YOU TAKE TODAY TO ENSURE THAT YOU REACH YOUR BIG GOAL?

1 _____

2 _____

3 _____

■ MORNING RITUAL

SUCCESS STARTS IN THE HABITS YOU CREATE FROM THE TIME YOU WAKE UP. HOW WILL YOU PREPARE YOUR MIND FOR ACTION TODAY?

I WILL _____

I WILL _____

I WILL _____

■ GRATITUDE

PEOPLE WHO PRACTICE THE HABIT OF GRATITUDE ATTRACT MORE SUCCESS. WHO OR WHAT ARE YOU GRATEFUL FOR TODAY?

_____   _____

_____   _____

_____   _____

DAY ____

FACEBOOK CHECK-IN
COMMENT ON TODAY'S POST IN THE **RE-INVENT 360 JOURNAL COMMUNITY** FACEBOOK GROUP.

■ FITNESS FOCUS
A HEALTHY MIND IN A HEALTHY BODY. WHAT WILL YOU DO TODAY TO STAY ACTIVE?

_____

■ CONNECTING
WHO WILL YOU TALK TO TODAY TO GET YOU ONE STEP CLOSER TOWARDS REACHING YOUR GOAL?

_____

_____

■ TODAY'S WINS
NOW THAT THE DAY IS OVER, REFLECT ON WHAT YOU DID TODAY THAT HELPED YOU TO GET CLOSER TO YOUR BIG GOAL

_____   _____

_____   _____

■ PUSHING BEYOND
WHAT CAN YOU DO TOMORRROW TO IMPROVE ON THE LESSONS THAT YOU LEARNED TODAY?

_____

_____

_____

DAY ____

" *Believe you can and you're halfway there.*
— Theodore Roosevelt

■ THE BIG GOAL

WHAT WILL YOU ACHIEVE TODAY TO GET YOU ONE STEP CLOSER TO
ACHIEVING YOUR DREAM?

_____

_____

■ TAKING ACTION

WHAT STEPS WILL YOU TAKE TODAY TO ENSURE THAT YOU REACH
YOUR BIG GOAL?

1 _____

2 _____

3 _____

■ MORNING RITUAL

SUCCESS STARTS IN THE HABITS YOU CREATE FROM THE TIME YOU
WAKE UP. HOW WILL YOU PREPARE YOUR MIND FOR ACTION TODAY?

I WILL _____

I WILL _____

I WILL _____

■ GRATITUDE

PEOPLE WHO PRACTICE THE HABIT OF GRATITUDE ATTRACT MORE
SUCCESS. WHO OR WHAT ARE YOU GRATEFUL FOR TODAY?

_____   _____

_____   _____

_____   _____

DAY ____

FACEBOOK CHECK-IN

COMMENT ON TODAY'S POST IN THE **RE-INVENT 360 JOURNAL COMMUNITY** FACEBOOK GROUP.

■ FITNESS FOCUS

A HEALTHY MIND IN A HEALTHY BODY. WHAT WILL YOU DO TODAY TO STAY ACTIVE?

_____

■ CONNECTING

WHO WILL YOU TALK TO TODAY TO GET YOU ONE STEP CLOSER TOWARDS REACHING YOUR GOAL?

_____

_____

((EVENING REFLECTION

■ TODAY'S WINS

NOW THAT THE DAY IS OVER, REFLECT ON WHAT YOU DID TODAY THAT HELPED YOU TO GET CLOSER TO YOUR BIG GOAL

_____   _____

_____   _____

■ PUSHING BEYOND

WHAT CAN YOU DO TOMORRROW TO IMPROVE ON THE LESSONS THAT YOU LEARNED TODAY?

_____

_____

_____

30

DAY _____

> *You cant win if you don't begin. — Robin Sharma*

THE BIG GOAL

WHAT WILL YOU ACHIEVE TODAY TO GET YOU ONE STEP CLOSER TO ACHIEVING YOUR DREAM?

_____

_____

TAKING ACTION

WHAT STEPS WILL YOU TAKE TODAY TO ENSURE THAT YOU REACH YOUR BIG GOAL?

_____

_____

_____

MORNING RITUAL

SUCCESS STARTS IN THE HABITS YOU CREATE FROM THE TIME YOU WAKE UP. HOW WILL YOU PREPARE YOUR MIND FOR ACTION TODAY?

I WILL _____

I WILL _____

I WILL _____

GRATITUDE

PEOPLE WHO PRACTICE THE HABIT OF GRATITUDE ATTRACT MORE SUCCESS. WHO OR WHAT ARE YOU GRATEFUL FOR TODAY?

_____   _____

_____   _____

_____   _____

DAY _____

FACEBOOK CHECK-IN
COMMENT ON TODAY'S POST IN THE **RE-INVENT 360 JOURNAL COMMUNITY** FACEBOOK GROUP.

■ FITNESS FOCUS
A HEALTHY MIND IN A HEALTHY BODY. WHAT WILL YOU DO TODAY TO STAY ACTIVE?

_____

■ CONNECTING
WHO WILL YOU TALK TO TODAY TO GET YOU ONE STEP CLOSER TOWARDS REACHING YOUR GOAL?

_____

_____

(EVENING REFLECTION

■ TODAY'S WINS
NOW THAT THE DAY IS OVER, REFLECT ON WHAT YOU DID TODAY THAT HELPED YOU TO GET CLOSER TO YOUR BIG GOAL

_____   _____

_____   _____

■ PUSHING BEYOND
WHAT CAN YOU DO TOMORRROW TO IMPROVE ON THE LESSONS THAT YOU LEARNED TODAY?

_____

_____

_____

DAY ____

> ❝ *Life is a mirror of your consistent thoughts.*
> *— Napoleon Hill*

▊ THE BIG GOAL

WHAT WILL YOU ACHIEVE TODAY TO GET YOU ONE STEP CLOSER TO ACHIEVING YOUR DREAM?

_____

_____

▊ TAKING ACTION

WHAT STEPS WILL YOU TAKE TODAY TO ENSURE THAT YOU REACH YOUR BIG GOAL?

_____

_____

_____

_____

▊ MORNING RITUAL

SUCCESS STARTS IN THE HABITS YOU CREATE FROM THE TIME YOU WAKE UP. HOW WILL YOU PREPARE YOUR MIND FOR ACTION TODAY?

I WILL _____

I WILL _____

I WILL _____

▊ GRATITUDE

PEOPLE WHO PRACTICE THE HABIT OF GRATITUDE ATTRACT MORE SUCCESS. WHO OR WHAT ARE YOU GRATEFUL FOR TODAY?

_____   _____

_____   _____

_____   _____

DAY ____

 **FACEBOOK CHECK-IN**
COMMENT ON TODAY'S POST IN THE **RE-INVENT 360 JOURNAL COMMUNITY** FACEBOOK GROUP.

■ FITNESS FOCUS
A HEALTHY MIND IN A HEALTHY BODY. WHAT WILL YOU DO TODAY TO STAY ACTIVE?

_____

■ CONNECTING
WHO WILL YOU TALK TO TODAY TO GET YOU ONE STEP CLOSER TOWARDS REACHING YOUR GOAL?

_____

_____

☾ EVENING REFLECTION

■ TODAY'S WINS
NOW THAT THE DAY IS OVER, REFLECT ON WHAT YOU DID TODAY THAT HELPED YOU TO GET CLOSER TO YOUR BIG GOAL

_____ _____

_____ _____

■ PUSHING BEYOND
WHAT CAN YOU DO TOMORRROW TO IMPROVE ON THE LESSONS THAT YOU LEARNED TODAY?

_____

_____

_____

DAY ____

❝ *Peace comes from within. Do not seek it without.*
— Buddha

■ THE BIG GOAL

WHAT WILL YOU ACHIEVE TODAY TO GET YOU ONE STEP CLOSER TO ACHIEVING YOUR DREAM?

_____

_____

■ TAKING ACTION

WHAT STEPS WILL YOU TAKE TODAY TO ENSURE THAT YOU REACH YOUR BIG GOAL?

1 _____

2 _____

3 _____

■ MORNING RITUAL

SUCCESS STARTS IN THE HABITS YOU CREATE FROM THE TIME YOU WAKE UP. HOW WILL YOU PREPARE YOUR MIND FOR ACTION TODAY?

I WILL _____

I WILL _____

I WILL _____

■ GRATITUDE

PEOPLE WHO PRACTICE THE HABIT OF GRATITUDE ATTRACT MORE SUCCESS. WHO OR WHAT ARE YOU GRATEFUL FOR TODAY?

_____   _____

_____   _____

_____   _____

DAY ____

FACEBOOK CHECK-IN
COMMENT ON TODAY'S POST IN THE **RE-INVENT 360 JOURNAL COMMUNITY** FACEBOOK GROUP.

■ FITNESS FOCUS
A HEALTHY MIND IN A HEALTHY BODY. WHAT WILL YOU DO TODAY TO STAY ACTIVE?

_____

■ CONNECTING
WHO WILL YOU TALK TO TODAY TO GET YOU ONE STEP CLOSER TOWARDS REACHING YOUR GOAL?

_____

_____

☾ EVENING REFLECTION

■ TODAY'S WINS
NOW THAT THE DAY IS OVER, REFLECT ON WHAT YOU DID TODAY THAT HELPED YOU TO GET CLOSER TO YOUR BIG GOAL

_____   _____

_____   _____

■ PUSHING BEYOND
WHAT CAN YOU DO TOMORROW TO IMPROVE ON THE LESSONS THAT YOU LEARNED TODAY?

_____

_____

_____

DAY ____

DATE _____

> *Persistence and determination alone are omnipotent.*
> *— Calvin Coolidge*

■ THE BIG GOAL

WHAT WILL YOU ACHIEVE TODAY TO GET YOU ONE STEP CLOSER TO ACHIEVING YOUR DREAM?

_____

_____

■ TAKING ACTION

WHAT STEPS WILL YOU TAKE TODAY TO ENSURE THAT YOU REACH YOUR BIG GOAL?

_____

_____

_____

■ MORNING RITUAL

SUCCESS STARTS IN THE HABITS YOU CREATE FROM THE TIME YOU WAKE UP. HOW WILL YOU PREPARE YOUR MIND FOR ACTION TODAY?

I WILL _____

I WILL _____

I WILL _____

■ GRATITUDE

PEOPLE WHO PRACTICE THE HABIT OF GRATITUDE ATTRACT MORE SUCCESS. WHO OR WHAT ARE YOU GRATEFUL FOR TODAY?

_____   _____

_____   _____

_____   _____

DAY ____

FACEBOOK CHECK-IN
COMMENT ON TODAY'S POST IN THE **RE-INVENT 360 JOURNAL COMMUNITY** FACEBOOK GROUP.

■ FITNESS FOCUS
A HEALTHY MIND IN A HEALTHY BODY. WHAT WILL YOU DO TODAY TO STAY ACTIVE?

_____

■ CONNECTING
WHO WILL YOU TALK TO TODAY TO GET YOU ONE STEP CLOSER TOWARDS REACHING YOUR GOAL?

_____

_____

☾ EVENING REFLECTION

■ TODAY'S WINS
NOW THAT THE DAY IS OVER, REFLECT ON WHAT YOU DID TODAY THAT HELPED YOU TO GET CLOSER TO YOUR BIG GOAL

_____   _____

_____   _____

■ PUSHING BEYOND
WHAT CAN YOU DO TOMORRROW TO IMPROVE ON THE LESSONS THAT YOU LEARNED TODAY?

_____

_____

_____

DAY ____

> ❝ *Trade your expectation for appreciation and the world changes instantly. — Tony Robbins*

■ THE BIG GOAL

WHAT WILL YOU ACHIEVE TODAY TO GET YOU ONE STEP CLOSER TO ACHIEVING YOUR DREAM?

_____

_____

■ TAKING ACTION

WHAT STEPS WILL YOU TAKE TODAY TO ENSURE THAT YOU REACH YOUR BIG GOAL?

1. _____

2. _____

3. _____

■ MORNING RITUAL

SUCCESS STARTS IN THE HABITS YOU CREATE FROM THE TIME YOU WAKE UP. HOW WILL YOU PREPARE YOUR MIND FOR ACTION TODAY?

I WILL _____

I WILL _____

I WILL _____

■ GRATITUDE

PEOPLE WHO PRACTICE THE HABIT OF GRATITUDE ATTRACT MORE SUCCESS. WHO OR WHAT ARE YOU GRATEFUL FOR TODAY?

_____   _____

_____   _____

_____   _____

DAY ____

FACEBOOK CHECK-IN

COMMENT ON TODAY'S POST IN THE **RE-INVENT 360 JOURNAL COMMUNITY** FACEBOOK GROUP.

■ FITNESS FOCUS

A HEALTHY MIND IN A HEALTHY BODY. WHAT WILL YOU DO TODAY TO STAY ACTIVE?

_____

■ CONNECTING

WHO WILL YOU TALK TO TODAY TO GET YOU ONE STEP CLOSER TOWARDS REACHING YOUR GOAL?

_____

_____

EVENING REFLECTION

■ TODAY'S WINS

NOW THAT THE DAY IS OVER, REFLECT ON WHAT YOU DID TODAY THAT HELPED YOU TO GET CLOSER TO YOUR BIG GOAL

_____   _____

_____   _____

■ PUSHING BEYOND

WHAT CAN YOU DO TOMORRROW TO IMPROVE ON THE LESSONS THAT YOU LEARNED TODAY?

_____

_____

_____

DAY ____

> *" Once you make a decision, the universe conspires to make it happen." — Ralph Waldo Emerson*

■ THE BIG GOAL

WHAT WILL YOU ACHIEVE TODAY TO GET YOU ONE STEP CLOSER TO ACHIEVING YOUR DREAM?

_____

_____

■ TAKING ACTION

WHAT STEPS WILL YOU TAKE TODAY TO ENSURE THAT YOU REACH YOUR BIG GOAL?

1 _____

2 _____

3 _____

■ MORNING RITUAL

SUCCESS STARTS IN THE HABITS YOU CREATE FROM THE TIME YOU WAKE UP. HOW WILL YOU PREPARE YOUR MIND FOR ACTION TODAY?

I WILL _____

I WILL _____

I WILL _____

■ GRATITUDE

PEOPLE WHO PRACTICE THE HABIT OF GRATITUDE ATTRACT MORE SUCCESS. WHO OR WHAT ARE YOU GRATEFUL FOR TODAY?

_____   _____

_____   _____

_____   _____

DAY ____

FACEBOOK CHECK-IN

COMMENT ON TODAY'S POST IN THE **RE-INVENT 360 JOURNAL COMMUNITY** FACEBOOK GROUP.

■ FITNESS FOCUS

A HEALTHY MIND IN A HEALTHY BODY. WHAT WILL YOU DO TODAY TO STAY ACTIVE?

_____

■ CONNECTING

WHO WILL YOU TALK TO TODAY TO GET YOU ONE STEP CLOSER TOWARDS REACHING YOUR GOAL?

_____

_____

((EVENING REFLECTION

■ TODAY'S WINS

NOW THAT THE DAY IS OVER, REFLECT ON WHAT YOU DID TODAY THAT HELPED YOU TO GET CLOSER TO YOUR BIG GOAL

_____   _____

_____   _____

■ PUSHING BEYOND

WHAT CAN YOU DO TOMORROW TO IMPROVE ON THE LESSONS THAT YOU LEARNED TODAY?

_____

_____

_____

DAY ____

> ❝ *I can be changed by what happens to me but I refuse to be reduced by it. — Maya Angelou*

■ THE BIG GOAL

WHAT WILL YOU ACHIEVE TODAY TO GET YOU ONE STEP CLOSER TO ACHIEVING YOUR DREAM?

_____

_____

■ TAKING ACTION

WHAT STEPS WILL YOU TAKE TODAY TO ENSURE THAT YOU REACH YOUR BIG GOAL?

1. _____

2. _____

3. _____

■ MORNING RITUAL

SUCCESS STARTS IN THE HABITS YOU CREATE FROM THE TIME YOU WAKE UP. HOW WILL YOU PREPARE YOUR MIND FOR ACTION TODAY?

I WILL _____

I WILL _____

I WILL _____

■ GRATITUDE

PEOPLE WHO PRACTICE THE HABIT OF GRATITUDE ATTRACT MORE SUCCESS. WHO OR WHAT ARE YOU GRATEFUL FOR TODAY?

_____   _____

_____   _____

_____   _____

DAY ____

FACEBOOK CHECK-IN

COMMENT ON TODAY'S POST IN THE **RE-INVENT 360 JOURNAL COMMUNITY** FACEBOOK GROUP.

■ FITNESS FOCUS

A HEALTHY MIND IN A HEALTHY BODY. WHAT WILL YOU DO TODAY TO STAY ACTIVE?

_____

■ CONNECTING

WHO WILL YOU TALK TO TODAY TO GET YOU ONE STEP CLOSER TOWARDS REACHING YOUR GOAL?

_____

_____

☾ EVENING REFLECTION

■ TODAY'S WINS

NOW THAT THE DAY IS OVER, REFLECT ON WHAT YOU DID TODAY THAT HELPED YOU TO GET CLOSER TO YOUR BIG GOAL

_____   _____

_____   _____

■ PUSHING BEYOND

WHAT CAN YOU DO TOMORROW TO IMPROVE ON THE LESSONS THAT YOU LEARNED TODAY?

_____

_____

_____

DAY ____

" *If you get the inside right, the outside will fall into place.*
— Eckhart Tolle

■ THE BIG GOAL

WHAT WILL YOU ACHIEVE TODAY TO GET YOU ONE STEP CLOSER TO ACHIEVING YOUR DREAM?

_____

_____

■ TAKING ACTION

WHAT STEPS WILL YOU TAKE TODAY TO ENSURE THAT YOU REACH YOUR BIG GOAL?

1 _____

2 _____

3 _____

■ MORNING RITUAL

SUCCESS STARTS IN THE HABITS YOU CREATE FROM THE TIME YOU WAKE UP. HOW WILL YOU PREPARE YOUR MIND FOR ACTION TODAY?

I WILL _____

I WILL _____

I WILL _____

■ GRATITUDE

PEOPLE WHO PRACTICE THE HABIT OF GRATITUDE ATTRACT MORE SUCCESS. WHO OR WHAT ARE YOU GRATEFUL FOR TODAY?

_____   _____

_____   _____

_____   _____

DAY ____

FACEBOOK CHECK-IN

COMMENT ON TODAY'S POST IN THE **RE-INVENT 360 JOURNAL COMMUNITY** FACEBOOK GROUP.

■ FITNESS FOCUS

A HEALTHY MIND IN A HEALTHY BODY. WHAT WILL YOU DO TODAY TO STAY ACTIVE?

_____

■ CONNECTING

WHO WILL YOU TALK TO TODAY TO GET YOU ONE STEP CLOSER TOWARDS REACHING YOUR GOAL?

_____

_____

EVENING REFLECTION

■ TODAY'S WINS

NOW THAT THE DAY IS OVER, REFLECT ON WHAT YOU DID TODAY THAT HELPED YOU TO GET CLOSER TO YOUR BIG GOAL

_____   _____

_____   _____

■ PUSHING BEYOND

WHAT CAN YOU DO TOMORROW TO IMPROVE ON THE LESSONS THAT YOU LEARNED TODAY?

_____

_____

_____

46

10-DAY
CHECK IN

Your body is your temple.

SHAZ ALIDINA

10-DAY CHECK IN

■ THE BIG GOAL
HOW MUCH CLOSER ARE YOU TO YOUR GOAL?
(1 – NOT MUCH, 5 – MADE AVERAGE PROGRESS, 10 – BIG STEPS)

CIRCLE ONE: 1   2   3   4   5   6   7   8   9   10

HOW HAS YOUR VISION FOR YOUR BIG GOAL EXPANDED THIS WEEK?
_____
_____
_____

■ TAKING ACTION
WHAT ACTIONS DID YOU FEEL GREAT ABOUT THIS WEEK?
_____
_____
_____

■ MORNING RITUAL
HOW MANY DAYS DID YOU PERFORM YOUR MORNING RITUAL?

CIRCLE ONE: 1   2   3   4   5   6   7   8   9   10

WHICH ACTIVITIES SERVED YOU ESPECIALLY WELL?
_____
_____
_____

■ GRATITUDE
WHICH OF YOUR BIG WINS THIS WEEK ARE YOU MOST GRATEFUL FOR?
_____
_____

HOW CAN YOU BUILD ON THIS WIN?
_____
_____

10-DAY CHECK IN

■ FITNESS
HOW MANY DAYS DID YOU GET ACTIVE DURING THIS CYCLE?

CIRCLE ONE: 1   2   3   4   5   6   7   8   9   10

IF LESS THAN 5, WHAT CHANGES DO YOU NEED TO MAKE TO CREATE TIME FOR YOUR HEALTH?

_____

_____

■ CONNECTING
HOW MANY CONNECTIONS DID YOU MAKE THIS WEEK?

CIRCLE ONE: 1   2   3   4   5   6   7   8   9   10

WHICH PERSON PROVED TO BE AN INVALUABLE CONNECTION IN GETTING YOU CLOSER TO YOUR BIG GOAL?

_____

WHAT CAN YOU DO TO IN TURN TO BE AN ASSET TO THEM?

_____

_____

■ MIND DUMP!
SCRIBBLE OUT EVERYTHING THAT'S ON YOUR MIND AS YOU LOOK TOWARDS THE NEXT 10 DAYS. WHAT NEEDS TO BE DONE? WHO NEEDS TO BE CONTACTED? WHAT TOOLS DO YOU NEED? WRITE. DRAW. DOODLE.

READY. SET.
GO!

DAY ____

DATE _____

" *A ship is always safe at shore but that is not what it's built for.* — *Albert Einstein*

■ THE BIG GOAL

WHAT WILL YOU ACHIEVE TODAY TO GET YOU ONE STEP CLOSER TO ACHIEVING YOUR DREAM?

_____

_____

■ TAKING ACTION

WHAT STEPS WILL YOU TAKE TODAY TO ENSURE THAT YOU REACH YOUR BIG GOAL?

1 _____

2 _____

3 _____

■ MORNING RITUAL

SUCCESS STARTS IN THE HABITS YOU CREATE FROM THE TIME YOU WAKE UP. HOW WILL YOU PREPARE YOUR MIND FOR ACTION TODAY?

I WILL _____

I WILL _____

I WILL _____

■ GRATITUDE

PEOPLE WHO PRACTICE THE HABIT OF GRATITUDE ATTRACT MORE SUCCESS. WHO OR WHAT ARE YOU GRATEFUL FOR TODAY?

_____   _____

_____   _____

_____   _____

DAY _____

FACEBOOK CHECK-IN
COMMENT ON TODAY'S POST IN THE **RE-INVENT 360 JOURNAL COMMUNITY** FACEBOOK GROUP.

■ FITNESS FOCUS
A HEALTHY MIND IN A HEALTHY BODY. WHAT WILL YOU DO TODAY TO STAY ACTIVE?

_____

■ CONNECTING
WHO WILL YOU TALK TO TODAY TO GET YOU ONE STEP CLOSER TOWARDS REACHING YOUR GOAL?

_____

_____

■ TODAY'S WINS
NOW THAT THE DAY IS OVER, REFLECT ON WHAT YOU DID TODAY THAT HELPED YOU TO GET CLOSER TO YOUR BIG GOAL

_____   _____

_____   _____

■ PUSHING BEYOND
WHAT CAN YOU DO TOMORROW TO IMPROVE ON THE LESSONS THAT YOU LEARNED TODAY?

_____

_____

_____

_____

DAY ____

DATE _____

> *"Unless you try to do something beyond what you have already mastered, you will never grow. — Ronald Osborn*

■ THE BIG GOAL

WHAT WILL YOU ACHIEVE TODAY TO GET YOU ONE STEP CLOSER TO ACHIEVING YOUR DREAM?

_____

_____

■ TAKING ACTION

WHAT STEPS WILL YOU TAKE TODAY TO ENSURE THAT YOU REACH YOUR BIG GOAL?

1 _____

2 _____

3 _____

■ MORNING RITUAL

SUCCESS STARTS IN THE HABITS YOU CREATE FROM THE TIME YOU WAKE UP. HOW WILL YOU PREPARE YOUR MIND FOR ACTION TODAY?

I WILL _____

I WILL _____

I WILL _____

■ GRATITUDE

PEOPLE WHO PRACTICE THE HABIT OF GRATITUDE ATTRACT MORE SUCCESS. WHO OR WHAT ARE YOU GRATEFUL FOR TODAY?

_____   _____

_____   _____

_____   _____

DAY ____

FACEBOOK CHECK-IN
COMMENT ON TODAY'S POST IN THE **RE-INVENT 360 JOURNAL COMMUNITY** FACEBOOK GROUP.

■ FITNESS FOCUS
A HEALTHY MIND IN A HEALTHY BODY. WHAT WILL YOU DO TODAY TO STAY ACTIVE?

■ CONNECTING
WHO WILL YOU TALK TO TODAY TO GET YOU ONE STEP CLOSER TOWARDS REACHING YOUR GOAL?

☾ EVENING REFLECTION

■ TODAY'S WINS
NOW THAT THE DAY IS OVER, REFLECT ON WHAT YOU DID TODAY THAT HELPED YOU TO GET CLOSER TO YOUR BIG GOAL

■ PUSHING BEYOND
WHAT CAN YOU DO TOMORRROW TO IMPROVE ON THE LESSONS THAT YOU LEARNED TODAY?

DAY ____

> ❝ *When you no longer split your flow of energy with contradictory thoughts, you will know your power.*
> *— Abraham Hicks*

■ THE BIG GOAL

WHAT WILL YOU ACHIEVE TODAY TO GET YOU ONE STEP CLOSER TO ACHIEVING YOUR DREAM?

_____

_____

■ TAKING ACTION

WHAT STEPS WILL YOU TAKE TODAY TO ENSURE THAT YOU REACH YOUR BIG GOAL?

1 _____

2 _____

3 _____

■ MORNING RITUAL

SUCCESS STARTS IN THE HABITS YOU CREATE FROM THE TIME YOU WAKE UP. HOW WILL YOU PREPARE YOUR MIND FOR ACTION TODAY?

I WILL _____

I WILL _____

I WILL _____

■ GRATITUDE

PEOPLE WHO PRACTICE THE HABIT OF GRATITUDE ATTRACT MORE SUCCESS. WHO OR WHAT ARE YOU GRATEFUL FOR TODAY?

_____   _____

_____   _____

_____   _____

DAY ____

FACEBOOK CHECK-IN
COMMENT ON TODAY'S POST IN THE **RE-INVENT 360 JOURNAL COMMUNITY** FACEBOOK GROUP.

■ FITNESS FOCUS
A HEALTHY MIND IN A HEALTHY BODY. WHAT WILL YOU DO TODAY TO STAY ACTIVE?

_____

■ CONNECTING
WHO WILL YOU TALK TO TODAY TO GET YOU ONE STEP CLOSER TOWARDS REACHING YOUR GOAL?

_____

_____

■ TODAY'S WINS
NOW THAT THE DAY IS OVER, REFLECT ON WHAT YOU DID TODAY THAT HELPED YOU TO GET CLOSER TO YOUR BIG GOAL

_____   _____

_____   _____

■ PUSHING BEYOND
WHAT CAN YOU DO TOMORRROW TO IMPROVE ON THE LESSONS THAT YOU LEARNED TODAY?

_____

_____

_____

DAY ____

> ❝ *Let yourself be silently drawn by the strange pull of what you really love. It will not lead you astray. — Rumi*

■ THE BIG GOAL

WHAT WILL YOU ACHIEVE TODAY TO GET YOU ONE STEP CLOSER TO ACHIEVING YOUR DREAM?

_____

_____

■ TAKING ACTION

WHAT STEPS WILL YOU TAKE TODAY TO ENSURE THAT YOU REACH YOUR BIG GOAL?

1 _____

2 _____

3 _____

■ MORNING RITUAL

SUCCESS STARTS IN THE HABITS YOU CREATE FROM THE TIME YOU WAKE UP. HOW WILL YOU PREPARE YOUR MIND FOR ACTION TODAY?

I WILL _____

I WILL _____

I WILL _____

■ GRATITUDE

PEOPLE WHO PRACTICE THE HABIT OF GRATITUDE ATTRACT MORE SUCCESS. WHO OR WHAT ARE YOU GRATEFUL FOR TODAY?

_____   _____

_____   _____

_____   _____

DAY ____

FACEBOOK CHECK-IN

COMMENT ON TODAY'S POST IN THE **RE-INVENT 360 JOURNAL COMMUNITY** FACEBOOK GROUP.

■ FITNESS FOCUS

A HEALTHY MIND IN A HEALTHY BODY. WHAT WILL YOU DO TODAY TO STAY ACTIVE?

■ CONNECTING

WHO WILL YOU TALK TO TODAY TO GET YOU ONE STEP CLOSER TOWARDS REACHING YOUR GOAL?

☾ EVENING REFLECTION

■ TODAY'S WINS

NOW THAT THE DAY IS OVER, REFLECT ON WHAT YOU DID TODAY THAT HELPED YOU TO GET CLOSER TO YOUR BIG GOAL

■ PUSHING BEYOND

WHAT CAN YOU DO TOMORRROW TO IMPROVE ON THE LESSONS THAT YOU LEARNED TODAY?

DAY ____

DATE _____

> **"** *You yourself are your own obstacle, rise above yourself.*
> *— Hafiz*

■ THE BIG GOAL

WHAT WILL YOU ACHIEVE TODAY TO GET YOU ONE STEP CLOSER TO ACHIEVING YOUR DREAM?

_____

_____

■ TAKING ACTION

WHAT STEPS WILL YOU TAKE TODAY TO ENSURE THAT YOU REACH YOUR BIG GOAL?

1 _____

2 _____

3 _____

■ MORNING RITUAL

SUCCESS STARTS IN THE HABITS YOU CREATE FROM THE TIME YOU WAKE UP. HOW WILL YOU PREPARE YOUR MIND FOR ACTION TODAY?

I WILL _____

I WILL _____

I WILL _____

■ GRATITUDE

PEOPLE WHO PRACTICE THE HABIT OF GRATITUDE ATTRACT MORE SUCCESS. WHO OR WHAT ARE YOU GRATEFUL FOR TODAY?

_____   _____

_____   _____

_____   _____

FACEBOOK CHECK-IN
COMMENT ON TODAY'S POST IN THE **RE-INVENT 360 JOURNAL COMMUNITY** FACEBOOK GROUP.

■ FITNESS FOCUS
A HEALTHY MIND IN A HEALTHY BODY. WHAT WILL YOU DO TODAY TO STAY ACTIVE?

_____

■ CONNECTING
WHO WILL YOU TALK TO TODAY TO GET YOU ONE STEP CLOSER TOWARDS REACHING YOUR GOAL?

_____

_____

EVENING REFLECTION

■ TODAY'S WINS
NOW THAT THE DAY IS OVER, REFLECT ON WHAT YOU DID TODAY THAT HELPED YOU TO GET CLOSER TO YOUR BIG GOAL

_____   _____

_____   _____

■ PUSHING BEYOND
WHAT CAN YOU DO TOMORRROW TO IMPROVE ON THE LESSONS THAT YOU LEARNED TODAY?

_____

_____

_____

DAY _____

❝ *No one can make you feel inferior without your consent.*
— Eleanor Roosevelt

■ THE BIG GOAL

WHAT WILL YOU ACHIEVE TODAY TO GET YOU ONE STEP CLOSER TO
ACHIEVING YOUR DREAM?

_____

_____

■ TAKING ACTION

WHAT STEPS WILL YOU TAKE TODAY TO ENSURE THAT YOU REACH
YOUR BIG GOAL?

_____

_____

_____

■ MORNING RITUAL

SUCCESS STARTS IN THE HABITS YOU CREATE FROM THE TIME YOU
WAKE UP. HOW WILL YOU PREPARE YOUR MIND FOR ACTION TODAY?

I WILL _____

I WILL _____

I WILL _____

■ GRATITUDE

PEOPLE WHO PRACTICE THE HABIT OF GRATITUDE ATTRACT MORE
SUCCESS. WHO OR WHAT ARE YOU GRATEFUL FOR TODAY?

_____   _____

_____   _____

_____   _____

DAY ____

FACEBOOK CHECK-IN

COMMENT ON TODAY'S POST IN THE **RE-INVENT 360 JOURNAL COMMUNITY** FACEBOOK GROUP.

■ FITNESS FOCUS

A HEALTHY MIND IN A HEALTHY BODY. WHAT WILL YOU DO TODAY TO STAY ACTIVE?

_____

■ CONNECTING

WHO WILL YOU TALK TO TODAY TO GET YOU ONE STEP CLOSER TOWARDS REACHING YOUR GOAL?

_____

_____

EVENING REFLECTION

■ TODAY'S WINS

NOW THAT THE DAY IS OVER, REFLECT ON WHAT YOU DID TODAY THAT HELPED YOU TO GET CLOSER TO YOUR BIG GOAL

_____   _____

_____   _____

■ PUSHING BEYOND

WHAT CAN YOU DO TOMORRROW TO IMPROVE ON THE LESSONS THAT YOU LEARNED TODAY?

_____

_____

_____

DAY ____

> **"** *Faith is the art of holding on to things your reason has once accepted, in spite of your changing moods.*
> — *C.S. Lewis*

■ THE BIG GOAL

WHAT WILL YOU ACHIEVE TODAY TO GET YOU ONE STEP CLOSER TO ACHIEVING YOUR DREAM?

_____

_____

■ TAKING ACTION

WHAT STEPS WILL YOU TAKE TODAY TO ENSURE THAT YOU REACH YOUR BIG GOAL?

1 _____

2 _____

3 _____

■ MORNING RITUAL

SUCCESS STARTS IN THE HABITS YOU CREATE FROM THE TIME YOU WAKE UP. HOW WILL YOU PREPARE YOUR MIND FOR ACTION TODAY?

I WILL _____

I WILL _____

I WILL _____

■ GRATITUDE

PEOPLE WHO PRACTICE THE HABIT OF GRATITUDE ATTRACT MORE SUCCESS. WHO OR WHAT ARE YOU GRATEFUL FOR TODAY?

_____   _____

_____   _____

_____   _____

DAY ____

FACEBOOK CHECK-IN
COMMENT ON TODAY'S POST IN THE **RE-INVENT 360 JOURNAL COMMUNITY** FACEBOOK GROUP.

■ FITNESS FOCUS
A HEALTHY MIND IN A HEALTHY BODY. WHAT WILL YOU DO TODAY TO STAY ACTIVE?

_____

■ CONNECTING
WHO WILL YOU TALK TO TODAY TO GET YOU ONE STEP CLOSER TOWARDS REACHING YOUR GOAL?

_____

_____

☾ EVENING REFLECTION

■ TODAY'S WINS
NOW THAT THE DAY IS OVER, REFLECT ON WHAT YOU DID TODAY THAT HELPED YOU TO GET CLOSER TO YOUR BIG GOAL

_____   _____

_____   _____

■ PUSHING BEYOND
WHAT CAN YOU DO TOMORROW TO IMPROVE ON THE LESSONS THAT YOU LEARNED TODAY?

_____

_____

_____

DAY ____

 *Everything that irritates us about others can lead us to an understanding of ourselves. — Carl Jung*

■ THE BIG GOAL

WHAT WILL YOU ACHIEVE TODAY TO GET YOU ONE STEP CLOSER TO ACHIEVING YOUR DREAM?

_____

_____

■ TAKING ACTION

WHAT STEPS WILL YOU TAKE TODAY TO ENSURE THAT YOU REACH YOUR BIG GOAL?

_____

_____

_____

■ MORNING RITUAL

SUCCESS STARTS IN THE HABITS YOU CREATE FROM THE TIME YOU WAKE UP. HOW WILL YOU PREPARE YOUR MIND FOR ACTION TODAY?

I WILL _____

I WILL _____

I WILL _____

■ GRATITUDE

PEOPLE WHO PRACTICE THE HABIT OF GRATITUDE ATTRACT MORE SUCCESS. WHO OR WHAT ARE YOU GRATEFUL FOR TODAY?

_____   _____

_____   _____

_____   _____

DAY ____

 ## FACEBOOK CHECK-IN
COMMENT ON TODAY'S POST IN THE **RE-INVENT 360 JOURNAL COMMUNITY** FACEBOOK GROUP.

■ FITNESS FOCUS
A HEALTHY MIND IN A HEALTHY BODY. WHAT WILL YOU DO TODAY TO STAY ACTIVE?

_____

■ CONNECTING
WHO WILL YOU TALK TO TODAY TO GET YOU ONE STEP CLOSER TOWARDS REACHING YOUR GOAL?

_____

_____

 # EVENING REFLECTION

■ TODAY'S WINS
NOW THAT THE DAY IS OVER, REFLECT ON WHAT YOU DID TODAY THAT HELPED YOU TO GET CLOSER TO YOUR BIG GOAL

_____   _____

_____   _____

■ PUSHING BEYOND
WHAT CAN YOU DO TOMORRROW TO IMPROVE ON THE LESSONS THAT YOU LEARNED TODAY?

_____

_____

_____

DAY ____

> *You can't reach for anything new if your hands are still full of yesterday's junk. — Louise Smith*

THE BIG GOAL

WHAT WILL YOU ACHIEVE TODAY TO GET YOU ONE STEP CLOSER TO ACHIEVING YOUR DREAM?

_____

_____

TAKING ACTION

WHAT STEPS WILL YOU TAKE TODAY TO ENSURE THAT YOU REACH YOUR BIG GOAL?

1 _____

2 _____

3 _____

MORNING RITUAL

SUCCESS STARTS IN THE HABITS YOU CREATE FROM THE TIME YOU WAKE UP. HOW WILL YOU PREPARE YOUR MIND FOR ACTION TODAY?

I WILL _____

I WILL _____

I WILL _____

GRATITUDE

PEOPLE WHO PRACTICE THE HABIT OF GRATITUDE ATTRACT MORE SUCCESS. WHO OR WHAT ARE YOU GRATEFUL FOR TODAY?

_____   _____

_____   _____

_____   _____

FACEBOOK CHECK-IN

COMMENT ON TODAY'S POST IN THE **RE-INVENT 360 JOURNAL COMMUNITY** FACEBOOK GROUP.

■ FITNESS FOCUS

A HEALTHY MIND IN A HEALTHY BODY. WHAT WILL YOU DO TODAY TO STAY ACTIVE?

_____

■ CONNECTING

WHO WILL YOU TALK TO TODAY TO GET YOU ONE STEP CLOSER TOWARDS REACHING YOUR GOAL?

_____

_____

☽ EVENING REFLECTION

■ TODAY'S WINS

NOW THAT THE DAY IS OVER, REFLECT ON WHAT YOU DID TODAY THAT HELPED YOU TO GET CLOSER TO YOUR BIG GOAL

_____   _____

_____   _____

■ PUSHING BEYOND

WHAT CAN YOU DO TOMORRROW TO IMPROVE ON THE LESSONS THAT YOU LEARNED TODAY?

_____

_____

_____

DAY ____

DATE _____

> ❝ *I don't like to gamble, but if there's one thing I'm willing to bet on, it's myself.* — *Beyoncé Knowles-Carter*

■ THE BIG GOAL

WHAT WILL YOU ACHIEVE TODAY TO GET YOU ONE STEP CLOSER TO ACHIEVING YOUR DREAM?

_____

_____

■ TAKING ACTION

WHAT STEPS WILL YOU TAKE TODAY TO ENSURE THAT YOU REACH YOUR BIG GOAL?

_____

_____

_____

■ MORNING RITUAL

SUCCESS STARTS IN THE HABITS YOU CREATE FROM THE TIME YOU WAKE UP. HOW WILL YOU PREPARE YOUR MIND FOR ACTION TODAY?

WILL _____

WILL _____

WILL _____

■ GRATITUDE

PEOPLE WHO PRACTICE THE HABIT OF GRATITUDE ATTRACT MORE SUCCESS. WHO OR WHAT ARE YOU GRATEFUL FOR TODAY?

_____   _____

_____   _____

_____   _____

DAY ____

FACEBOOK CHECK-IN
COMMENT ON TODAY'S POST IN THE **RE-INVENT 360 JOURNAL COMMUNITY** FACEBOOK GROUP.

■ FITNESS FOCUS
A HEALTHY MIND IN A HEALTHY BODY. WHAT WILL YOU DO TODAY TO STAY ACTIVE?

_____

■ CONNECTING
WHO WILL YOU TALK TO TODAY TO GET YOU ONE STEP CLOSER TOWARDS REACHING YOUR GOAL?

_____

_____

☾ EVENING REFLECTION

■ TODAY'S WINS
NOW THAT THE DAY IS OVER, REFLECT ON WHAT YOU DID TODAY THAT HELPED YOU TO GET CLOSER TO YOUR BIG GOAL

_____   _____

_____   _____

■ PUSHING BEYOND
WHAT CAN YOU DO TOMORRROW TO IMPROVE ON THE LESSONS THAT YOU LEARNED TODAY?

_____

_____

_____

10-DAY
CHECK IN

" "

Rise above the horizon, let the light of your own divinity shine so bright that every path that seemed impossible starts lighting up with possibilities.

SHAZ ALIDINA

10-DAY CHECK IN

■ THE BIG GOAL
HOW MUCH CLOSER ARE YOU TO YOUR GOAL?
(1 – NOT MUCH, 5 – MADE AVERAGE PROGRESS, 10 – BIG STEPS)

CIRCLE ONE: 1   2   3   4   5   6   7   8   9   10

HOW HAS YOUR VISION FOR YOUR BIG GOAL EXPANDED THIS WEEK?
_____
_____
_____

■ TAKING ACTION
WHAT ACTIONS DID YOU FEEL GREAT ABOUT THIS WEEK?
_____
_____
_____

■ MORNING RITUAL
HOW MANY DAYS DID YOU PERFORM YOUR MORNING RITUAL?

CIRCLE ONE: 1   2   3   4   5   6   7   8   9   10

WHICH ACTIVITIES SERVED YOU ESPECIALLY WELL?
_____
_____
_____

■ GRATITUDE
WHICH OF YOUR BIG WINS THIS WEEK ARE YOU MOST GRATEFUL FOR?
_____
_____

HOW CAN YOU BUILD ON THIS WIN?
_____
_____

10-DAY CHECK IN

■ FITNESS
HOW MANY DAYS DID YOU GET ACTIVE DURING THIS CYCLE?

CIRCLE ONE: 1   2   3   4   5   6   7   8   9   10

IF LESS THAN 5, WHAT CHANGES DO YOU NEED TO MAKE TO CREATE TIME FOR YOUR HEALTH?

_____

_____

■ CONNECTING
HOW MANY CONNECTIONS DID YOU MAKE THIS WEEK?

CIRCLE ONE: 1   2   3   4   5   6   7   8   9   10

WHICH PERSON PROVED TO BE AN INVALUABLE CONNECTION IN GET-TING YOU CLOSER TO YOUR BIG GOAL?

_____

WHAT CAN YOU DO TO IN TURN TO BE AN ASSET TO THEM?

_____

_____

■ MIND DUMP!
SCRIBBLE OUT EVERYTHING THAT'S ON YOUR MIND AS YOU LOOK TO-WARDS THE NEXT 10 DAYS. WHAT NEEDS TO BE DONE? WHO NEEDS TO BE CONTACTED? WHAT TOOLS DO YOU NEED? WRITE. DRAW. DOODLE.

READY. SET.
GO!

DAY ____

> " *Celebrate your success and stand strong when adversity hits, for when the storm clouds come in, the eagles soar while the small birds take cover. — Napoleon Hill*

◀ THE BIG GOAL

WHAT WILL YOU ACHIEVE TODAY TO GET YOU ONE STEP CLOSER TO ACHIEVING YOUR DREAM?

_____

_____

◀ TAKING ACTION

WHAT STEPS WILL YOU TAKE TODAY TO ENSURE THAT YOU REACH YOUR BIG GOAL?

1 _____

2 _____

3 _____

MORNING RITUAL

SUCCESS STARTS IN THE HABITS YOU CREATE FROM THE TIME YOU WAKE UP. HOW WILL YOU PREPARE YOUR MIND FOR ACTION TODAY?

I WILL _____

I WILL _____

I WILL _____

GRATITUDE

PEOPLE WHO PRACTICE THE HABIT OF GRATITUDE ATTRACT MORE SUCCESS. WHO OR WHAT ARE YOU GRATEFUL FOR TODAY?

_____   _____

_____   _____

_____   _____

DAY ____

FACEBOOK CHECK-IN

COMMENT ON TODAY'S POST IN THE **RE-INVENT 360 JOURNAL COMMUNITY** FACEBOOK GROUP.

■ FITNESS FOCUS

A HEALTHY MIND IN A HEALTHY BODY. WHAT WILL YOU DO TODAY TO STAY ACTIVE?

_____

■ CONNECTING

WHO WILL YOU TALK TO TODAY TO GET YOU ONE STEP CLOSER TOWARDS REACHING YOUR GOAL?

_____

_____

EVENING REFLECTION

■ TODAY'S WINS

NOW THAT THE DAY IS OVER, REFLECT ON WHAT YOU DID TODAY THAT HELPED YOU TO GET CLOSER TO YOUR BIG GOAL

_____   _____

_____   _____

■ PUSHING BEYOND

WHAT CAN YOU DO TOMORRROW TO IMPROVE ON THE LESSONS THAT YOU LEARNED TODAY?

_____

_____

_____

DAY _____

DATE _____

> *Make choices that are in alignment with who you are and where you want to see yourself in the future."*
> *— Jennifer O'Neill*

■ THE BIG GOAL

WHAT WILL YOU ACHIEVE TODAY TO GET YOU ONE STEP CLOSER TO ACHIEVING YOUR DREAM?

_____

_____

■ TAKING ACTION

WHAT STEPS WILL YOU TAKE TODAY TO ENSURE THAT YOU REACH YOUR BIG GOAL?

1 _____

2 _____

3 _____

■ MORNING RITUAL

SUCCESS STARTS IN THE HABITS YOU CREATE FROM THE TIME YOU WAKE UP. HOW WILL YOU PREPARE YOUR MIND FOR ACTION TODAY?

I WILL _____

I WILL _____

I WILL _____

■ GRATITUDE

PEOPLE WHO PRACTICE THE HABIT OF GRATITUDE ATTRACT MORE SUCCESS. WHO OR WHAT ARE YOU GRATEFUL FOR TODAY?

_____   _____

_____   _____

_____   _____

DAY ____

 ## FACEBOOK CHECK-IN
COMMENT ON TODAY'S POST IN THE **RE-INVENT 360 JOURNAL COMMUNITY** FACEBOOK GROUP.

■ FITNESS FOCUS
A HEALTHY MIND IN A HEALTHY BODY. WHAT WILL YOU DO TODAY TO STAY ACTIVE?

_____

■ CONNECTING
WHO WILL YOU TALK TO TODAY TO GET YOU ONE STEP CLOSER TOWARDS REACHING YOUR GOAL?

_____

_____

 # EVENING REFLECTION

■ TODAY'S WINS
NOW THAT THE DAY IS OVER, REFLECT ON WHAT YOU DID TODAY THAT HELPED YOU TO GET CLOSER TO YOUR BIG GOAL

_____   _____

_____   _____

■ PUSHING BEYOND
WHAT CAN YOU DO TOMORRROW TO IMPROVE ON THE LESSONS THAT YOU LEARNED TODAY?

_____

_____

_____

DAY ____

" *You are the average of the five people you spend the most time with.* — *Jim Rohn*

■ THE BIG GOAL

WHAT WILL YOU ACHIEVE TODAY TO GET YOU ONE STEP CLOSER TO ACHIEVING YOUR DREAM?

_____

_____

■ TAKING ACTION

WHAT STEPS WILL YOU TAKE TODAY TO ENSURE THAT YOU REACH YOUR BIG GOAL?

1 _____

2 _____

3 _____

■ MORNING RITUAL

SUCCESS STARTS IN THE HABITS YOU CREATE FROM THE TIME YOU WAKE UP. HOW WILL YOU PREPARE YOUR MIND FOR ACTION TODAY?

I WILL _____

I WILL _____

I WILL _____

■ GRATITUDE

PEOPLE WHO PRACTICE THE HABIT OF GRATITUDE ATTRACT MORE SUCCESS. WHO OR WHAT ARE YOU GRATEFUL FOR TODAY?

_____   _____

_____   _____

_____   _____

79

DAY _____

FACEBOOK CHECK-IN

COMMENT ON TODAY'S POST IN THE **RE-INVENT 360 JOURNAL COMMUNITY** FACEBOOK GROUP.

■ FITNESS FOCUS

A HEALTHY MIND IN A HEALTHY BODY. WHAT WILL YOU DO TODAY TO STAY ACTIVE?

■ CONNECTING

WHO WILL YOU TALK TO TODAY TO GET YOU ONE STEP CLOSER TOWARDS REACHING YOUR GOAL?

EVENING REFLECTION

■ TODAY'S WINS

NOW THAT THE DAY IS OVER, REFLECT ON WHAT YOU DID TODAY THAT HELPED YOU TO GET CLOSER TO YOUR BIG GOAL

■ PUSHING BEYOND

WHAT CAN YOU DO TOMORRROW TO IMPROVE ON THE LESSONS THAT YOU LEARNED TODAY?

DAY ____

" *A river cuts through rock, not because of its power, but because of its persistence. — Unknown*

■ THE BIG GOAL

WHAT WILL YOU ACHIEVE TODAY TO GET YOU ONE STEP CLOSER TO ACHIEVING YOUR DREAM?

_____

_____

■ TAKING ACTION

WHAT STEPS WILL YOU TAKE TODAY TO ENSURE THAT YOU REACH YOUR BIG GOAL?

1 _____

2 _____

3 _____

■ MORNING RITUAL

SUCCESS STARTS IN THE HABITS YOU CREATE FROM THE TIME YOU WAKE UP. HOW WILL YOU PREPARE YOUR MIND FOR ACTION TODAY?

I WILL _____

I WILL _____

I WILL _____

■ GRATITUDE

PEOPLE WHO PRACTICE THE HABIT OF GRATITUDE ATTRACT MORE SUCCESS. WHO OR WHAT ARE YOU GRATEFUL FOR TODAY?

_____   _____

_____   _____

_____   _____

DAY ____

FACEBOOK CHECK-IN
COMMENT ON TODAY'S POST IN THE **RE-INVENT 360 JOURNAL COMMUNITY** FACEBOOK GROUP.

■ FITNESS FOCUS
A HEALTHY MIND IN A HEALTHY BODY. WHAT WILL YOU DO TODAY TO STAY ACTIVE?

■ CONNECTING
WHO WILL YOU TALK TO TODAY TO GET YOU ONE STEP CLOSER TOWARDS REACHING YOUR GOAL?

EVENING REFLECTION

■ TODAY'S WINS
NOW THAT THE DAY IS OVER, REFLECT ON WHAT YOU DID TODAY THAT HELPED YOU TO GET CLOSER TO YOUR BIG GOAL

■ PUSHING BEYOND
WHAT CAN YOU DO TOMORRROW TO IMPROVE ON THE LESSONS THAT YOU LEARNED TODAY?

DAY ____

DATE _____

 Every minute spent worrying about the way things were is a moment stolen from creating the way things can be.
— Robin Sharma

■ THE BIG GOAL

WHAT WILL YOU ACHIEVE TODAY TO GET YOU ONE STEP CLOSER TO ACHIEVING YOUR DREAM?

_____

_____

■ TAKING ACTION

WHAT STEPS WILL YOU TAKE TODAY TO ENSURE THAT YOU REACH YOUR BIG GOAL?

1 _____

2 _____

3 _____

■ MORNING RITUAL

SUCCESS STARTS IN THE HABITS YOU CREATE FROM THE TIME YOU WAKE UP. HOW WILL YOU PREPARE YOUR MIND FOR ACTION TODAY?

I WILL _____

I WILL _____

I WILL _____

■ GRATITUDE

PEOPLE WHO PRACTICE THE HABIT OF GRATITUDE ATTRACT MORE SUCCESS. WHO OR WHAT ARE YOU GRATEFUL FOR TODAY?

_____   _____

_____   _____

_____   _____

ReInvent360Journal.com

FACEBOOK CHECK-IN
COMMENT ON TODAY'S POST IN THE **RE-INVENT 360 JOURNAL COMMUNITY** FACEBOOK GROUP.

■ FITNESS FOCUS
A HEALTHY MIND IN A HEALTHY BODY. WHAT WILL YOU DO TODAY TO STAY ACTIVE?

_____

■ CONNECTING
WHO WILL YOU TALK TO TODAY TO GET YOU ONE STEP CLOSER TOWARDS REACHING YOUR GOAL?

_____

_____

EVENING REFLECTION

■ TODAY'S WINS
NOW THAT THE DAY IS OVER, REFLECT ON WHAT YOU DID TODAY THAT HELPED YOU TO GET CLOSER TO YOUR BIG GOAL

_____   _____

_____   _____

■ PUSHING BEYOND
WHAT CAN YOU DO TOMORRROW TO IMPROVE ON THE LESSONS THAT YOU LEARNED TODAY?

_____

_____

_____

DAY ____

> " *Life is a gift, and it offers us the privilege, opportunity and responsibility to give something back by becoming more. —Tony Robbins*

■ THE BIG GOAL

WHAT WILL YOU ACHIEVE TODAY TO GET YOU ONE STEP CLOSER TO ACHIEVING YOUR DREAM?

_____

_____

■ TAKING ACTION

WHAT STEPS WILL YOU TAKE TODAY TO ENSURE THAT YOU REACH YOUR BIG GOAL?

1 _____

2 _____

3 _____

■ MORNING RITUAL

SUCCESS STARTS IN THE HABITS YOU CREATE FROM THE TIME YOU WAKE UP. HOW WILL YOU PREPARE YOUR MIND FOR ACTION TODAY?

I WILL _____

I WILL _____

I WILL _____

■ GRATITUDE

PEOPLE WHO PRACTICE THE HABIT OF GRATITUDE ATTRACT MORE SUCCESS. WHO OR WHAT ARE YOU GRATEFUL FOR TODAY?

_____   _____

_____   _____

_____   _____

DAY ___

FACEBOOK CHECK-IN
COMMENT ON TODAY'S POST IN THE **RE-INVENT 360 JOURNAL COMMUNITY** FACEBOOK GROUP.

■ FITNESS FOCUS
A HEALTHY MIND IN A HEALTHY BODY. WHAT WILL YOU DO TODAY TO STAY ACTIVE?

_____

■ CONNECTING
WHO WILL YOU TALK TO TODAY TO GET YOU ONE STEP CLOSER TOWARDS REACHING YOUR GOAL?

_____

_____

☽ EVENING REFLECTION

■ TODAY'S WINS
NOW THAT THE DAY IS OVER, REFLECT ON WHAT YOU DID TODAY THAT HELPED YOU TO GET CLOSER TO YOUR BIG GOAL

_____   _____

_____   _____

■ PUSHING BEYOND
WHAT CAN YOU DO TOMORRROW TO IMPROVE ON THE LESSONS THAT YOU LEARNED TODAY?

_____

_____

_____

DAY ____

DATE _____

> " *There is a huge amount of freedom that comes to you when you take nothing personally.* — Don Miguel Ruiz

■ THE BIG GOAL

WHAT WILL YOU ACHIEVE TODAY TO GET YOU ONE STEP CLOSER TO ACHIEVING YOUR DREAM?

_____

_____

■ TAKING ACTION

WHAT STEPS WILL YOU TAKE TODAY TO ENSURE THAT YOU REACH YOUR BIG GOAL?

1 _____

2 _____

3 _____

■ MORNING RITUAL

SUCCESS STARTS IN THE HABITS YOU CREATE FROM THE TIME YOU WAKE UP. HOW WILL YOU PREPARE YOUR MIND FOR ACTION TODAY?

I WILL _____

I WILL _____

I WILL _____

■ GRATITUDE

PEOPLE WHO PRACTICE THE HABIT OF GRATITUDE ATTRACT MORE SUCCESS. WHO OR WHAT ARE YOU GRATEFUL FOR TODAY?

_____   _____

_____   _____

_____   _____

87

DAY ____

FACEBOOK CHECK-IN
COMMENT ON TODAY'S POST IN THE **RE-INVENT 360 JOURNAL COMMUNITY** FACEBOOK GROUP.

■ FITNESS FOCUS
A HEALTHY MIND IN A HEALTHY BODY. WHAT WILL YOU DO TODAY TO STAY ACTIVE?

_____

■ CONNECTING
WHO WILL YOU TALK TO TODAY TO GET YOU ONE STEP CLOSER TOWARDS REACHING YOUR GOAL?

_____

_____

EVENING REFLECTION

■ TODAY'S WINS
NOW THAT THE DAY IS OVER, REFLECT ON WHAT YOU DID TODAY THAT HELPED YOU TO GET CLOSER TO YOUR BIG GOAL

_____   _____

_____   _____

■ PUSHING BEYOND
WHAT CAN YOU DO TOMORRROW TO IMPROVE ON THE LESSONS THAT YOU LEARNED TODAY?

_____

_____

_____

DAY ____

DATE _____

> " *Gratitude opens the door to... the power, the wisdom, the creativity of the Universe. You open the door through gratitude. — Deepak Chopra*

■ THE BIG GOAL

WHAT WILL YOU ACHIEVE TODAY TO GET YOU ONE STEP CLOSER TO ACHIEVING YOUR DREAM?

_____

_____

■ TAKING ACTION

WHAT STEPS WILL YOU TAKE TODAY TO ENSURE THAT YOU REACH YOUR BIG GOAL?

1 _____

2 _____

3 _____

■ MORNING RITUAL

SUCCESS STARTS IN THE HABITS YOU CREATE FROM THE TIME YOU WAKE UP. HOW WILL YOU PREPARE YOUR MIND FOR ACTION TODAY?

I WILL _____

I WILL _____

I WILL _____

■ GRATITUDE

PEOPLE WHO PRACTICE THE HABIT OF GRATITUDE ATTRACT MORE SUCCESS. WHO OR WHAT ARE YOU GRATEFUL FOR TODAY?

_____   _____

_____   _____

_____   _____

DAY ____

FACEBOOK CHECK-IN
COMMENT ON TODAY'S POST IN THE **RE-INVENT 360 JOURNAL COMMUNITY** FACEBOOK GROUP.

■ FITNESS FOCUS
A HEALTHY MIND IN A HEALTHY BODY. WHAT WILL YOU DO TODAY TO STAY ACTIVE?

_____

■ CONNECTING
WHO WILL YOU TALK TO TODAY TO GET YOU ONE STEP CLOSER TOWARDS REACHING YOUR GOAL?

_____

_____

EVENING REFLECTION

■ TODAY'S WINS
NOW THAT THE DAY IS OVER, REFLECT ON WHAT YOU DID TODAY THAT HELPED YOU TO GET CLOSER TO YOUR BIG GOAL

_____   _____

_____   _____

■ PUSHING BEYOND
WHAT CAN YOU DO TOMORRROW TO IMPROVE ON THE LESSONS THAT YOU LEARNED TODAY?

_____

_____

_____

_____

DAY _____

" *Everything has been created twice once on a mental plain and once on a physical plain. — Bob Proctor*

▮ THE BIG GOAL

WHAT WILL YOU ACHIEVE TODAY TO GET YOU ONE STEP CLOSER TO ACHIEVING YOUR DREAM?

_____

_____

▮ TAKING ACTION

WHAT STEPS WILL YOU TAKE TODAY TO ENSURE THAT YOU REACH YOUR BIG GOAL?

_____

_____

_____

▮ MORNING RITUAL

SUCCESS STARTS IN THE HABITS YOU CREATE FROM THE TIME YOU WAKE UP. HOW WILL YOU PREPARE YOUR MIND FOR ACTION TODAY?

I WILL _____

I WILL _____

I WILL _____

▮ GRATITUDE

PEOPLE WHO PRACTICE THE HABIT OF GRATITUDE ATTRACT MORE SUCCESS. WHO OR WHAT ARE YOU GRATEFUL FOR TODAY?

_____   _____

_____   _____

_____   _____

DAY ____

FACEBOOK CHECK-IN
COMMENT ON TODAY'S POST IN THE **RE-INVENT 360 JOURNAL COMMUNITY** FACEBOOK GROUP.

■ FITNESS FOCUS
A HEALTHY MIND IN A HEALTHY BODY. WHAT WILL YOU DO TODAY TO STAY ACTIVE?

_____

■ CONNECTING
WHO WILL YOU TALK TO TODAY TO GET YOU ONE STEP CLOSER TOWARDS REACHING YOUR GOAL?

_____

_____

EVENING REFLECTION

■ TODAY'S WINS
NOW THAT THE DAY IS OVER, REFLECT ON WHAT YOU DID TODAY THAT HELPED YOU TO GET CLOSER TO YOUR BIG GOAL

_____   _____

_____   _____

■ PUSHING BEYOND
WHAT CAN YOU DO TOMORRROW TO IMPROVE ON THE LESSONS THAT YOU LEARNED TODAY?

_____

_____

_____

DAY ____

DATE _____

> ❝ *When you immerse in the love within you, your world can't help but perfectly mirror it back.*
> — *Nicole Leigh West*

■ THE BIG GOAL

WHAT WILL YOU ACHIEVE TODAY TO GET YOU ONE STEP CLOSER TO ACHIEVING YOUR DREAM?

_____

_____

■ TAKING ACTION

WHAT STEPS WILL YOU TAKE TODAY TO ENSURE THAT YOU REACH YOUR BIG GOAL?

_____

_____

_____

■ MORNING RITUAL

SUCCESS STARTS IN THE HABITS YOU CREATE FROM THE TIME YOU WAKE UP. HOW WILL YOU PREPARE YOUR MIND FOR ACTION TODAY?

I WILL _____

I WILL _____

I WILL _____

■ GRATITUDE

PEOPLE WHO PRACTICE THE HABIT OF GRATITUDE ATTRACT MORE SUCCESS. WHO OR WHAT ARE YOU GRATEFUL FOR TODAY?

_____   _____

_____   _____

_____   _____

DAY ____

FACEBOOK CHECK-IN

COMMENT ON TODAY'S POST IN THE **RE-INVENT 360 JOURNAL COMMUNITY** FACEBOOK GROUP.

■ FITNESS FOCUS

A HEALTHY MIND IN A HEALTHY BODY. WHAT WILL YOU DO TODAY TO STAY ACTIVE?

_____

■ CONNECTING

WHO WILL YOU TALK TO TODAY TO GET YOU ONE STEP CLOSER TOWARDS REACHING YOUR GOAL?

_____

_____

☾ EVENING REFLECTION

■ TODAY'S WINS

NOW THAT THE DAY IS OVER, REFLECT ON WHAT YOU DID TODAY THAT HELPED YOU TO GET CLOSER TO YOUR BIG GOAL

_____   _____

_____   _____

■ PUSHING BEYOND

WHAT CAN YOU DO TOMORRROW TO IMPROVE ON THE LESSONS THAT YOU LEARNED TODAY?

_____

_____

_____

10-DAY
CHECK IN

Amplify your strengths.

SHAZ ALIDINA

10-DAY CHECK IN

■ THE BIG GOAL
HOW MUCH CLOSER ARE YOU TO YOUR GOAL?
(1 – NOT MUCH, 5 – MADE AVERAGE PROGRESS, 10 – BIG STEPS)

CIRCLE ONE: 1   2   3   4   5   6   7   8   9   10

HOW HAS YOUR VISION FOR YOUR BIG GOAL EXPANDED THIS WEEK?
_____
_____
_____

■ TAKING ACTION
WHAT ACTIONS DID YOU FEEL GREAT ABOUT THIS WEEK?
_____
_____
_____

■ MORNING RITUAL
HOW MANY DAYS DID YOU PERFORM YOUR MORNING RITUAL?

CIRCLE ONE: 1   2   3   4   5   6   7   8   9   10

WHICH ACTIVITIES SERVED YOU ESPECIALLY WELL?
_____
_____
_____

■ GRATITUDE
WHICH OF YOUR BIG WINS THIS WEEK ARE YOU MOST GRATEFUL FOR?
_____
_____

HOW CAN YOU BUILD ON THIS WIN?
_____
_____

10-DAY CHECK IN

■ FITNESS
HOW MANY DAYS DID YOU GET ACTIVE DURING THIS CYCLE?

CIRCLE ONE: 1   2   3   4   5   6   7   8   9   10

IF LESS THAN 5, WHAT CHANGES DO YOU NEED TO MAKE TO CREATE TIME FOR YOUR HEALTH?

_____

_____

■ CONNECTING
HOW MANY CONNECTIONS DID YOU MAKE THIS WEEK?

CIRCLE ONE: 1   2   3   4   5   6   7   8   9   10

WHICH PERSON PROVED TO BE AN INVALUABLE CONNECTION IN GET-TING YOU CLOSER TO YOUR BIG GOAL?

_____

WHAT CAN YOU DO TO IN TURN TO BE AN ASSET TO THEM?

_____

_____

■ MIND DUMP!
SCRIBBLE OUT EVERYTHING THAT'S ON YOUR MIND AS YOU LOOK TO-WARDS THE NEXT 10 DAYS. WHAT NEEDS TO BE DONE? WHO NEEDS TO BE CONTACTED? WHAT TOOLS DO YOU NEED? WRITE. DRAW. DOODLE.

READY. SET.
GO!

DAY ____

DATE _____

> *Take care of your body. It is the only place you have to live. — Jim Rohn*

◀ THE BIG GOAL

WHAT WILL YOU ACHIEVE TODAY TO GET YOU ONE STEP CLOSER TO ACHIEVING YOUR DREAM?

_____

_____

◀ TAKING ACTION

WHAT STEPS WILL YOU TAKE TODAY TO ENSURE THAT YOU REACH YOUR BIG GOAL?

_____

_____

_____

MORNING RITUAL

SUCCESS STARTS IN THE HABITS YOU CREATE FROM THE TIME YOU WAKE UP. HOW WILL YOU PREPARE YOUR MIND FOR ACTION TODAY?

I WILL _____

I WILL _____

I WILL _____

◀ GRATITUDE

PEOPLE WHO PRACTICE THE HABIT OF GRATITUDE ATTRACT MORE SUCCESS. WHO OR WHAT ARE YOU GRATEFUL FOR TODAY?

_____   _____

_____   _____

_____   _____

FACEBOOK CHECK-IN
COMMENT ON TODAY'S POST IN THE **RE-INVENT 360 JOURNAL COMMUNITY** FACEBOOK GROUP.

■ FITNESS FOCUS
A HEALTHY MIND IN A HEALTHY BODY. WHAT WILL YOU DO TODAY TO STAY ACTIVE?

_____

■ CONNECTING
WHO WILL YOU TALK TO TODAY TO GET YOU ONE STEP CLOSER TOWARDS REACHING YOUR GOAL?

_____

_____

((EVENING REFLECTION

■ TODAY'S WINS
NOW THAT THE DAY IS OVER, REFLECT ON WHAT YOU DID TODAY THAT HELPED YOU TO GET CLOSER TO YOUR BIG GOAL

_____   _____

_____   _____

■ PUSHING BEYOND
WHAT CAN YOU DO TOMORRROW TO IMPROVE ON THE LESSONS THAT YOU LEARNED TODAY?

_____

_____

_____

DAY ____

> ❝ *Without goals, and plans to reach them, you are like a ship that has set sail with no destination.*
> — *Fitzhugh Dodson*

▌ THE BIG GOAL

WHAT WILL YOU ACHIEVE TODAY TO GET YOU ONE STEP CLOSER TO ACHIEVING YOUR DREAM?

_____

_____

▌ TAKING ACTION

WHAT STEPS WILL YOU TAKE TODAY TO ENSURE THAT YOU REACH YOUR BIG GOAL?

_____

_____

_____

▌ MORNING RITUAL

SUCCESS STARTS IN THE HABITS YOU CREATE FROM THE TIME YOU WAKE UP. HOW WILL YOU PREPARE YOUR MIND FOR ACTION TODAY?

I WILL _____

I WILL _____

I WILL _____

▌ GRATITUDE

PEOPLE WHO PRACTICE THE HABIT OF GRATITUDE ATTRACT MORE SUCCESS. WHO OR WHAT ARE YOU GRATEFUL FOR TODAY?

_____   _____

_____   _____

_____   _____

DAY ____

FACEBOOK CHECK-IN
COMMENT ON TODAY'S POST IN THE **RE-INVENT 360 JOURNAL COMMUNITY** FACEBOOK GROUP.

■ FITNESS FOCUS
A HEALTHY MIND IN A HEALTHY BODY. WHAT WILL YOU DO TODAY TO STAY ACTIVE?

_____

■ CONNECTING
WHO WILL YOU TALK TO TODAY TO GET YOU ONE STEP CLOSER TOWARDS REACHING YOUR GOAL?

_____

_____

■ TODAY'S WINS
NOW THAT THE DAY IS OVER, REFLECT ON WHAT YOU DID TODAY THAT HELPED YOU TO GET CLOSER TO YOUR BIG GOAL

_____   _____

_____   _____

■ PUSHING BEYOND
WHAT CAN YOU DO TOMORROW TO IMPROVE ON THE LESSONS THAT YOU LEARNED TODAY?

_____

_____

_____

DAY ____

DATE _____

> ❝ *Every negative event contains within it the seed of an equal or greater benefit.* — *Napoleon Hill*

◼ THE BIG GOAL

WHAT WILL YOU ACHIEVE TODAY TO GET YOU ONE STEP CLOSER TO ACHIEVING YOUR DREAM?

_____

_____

◼ TAKING ACTION

WHAT STEPS WILL YOU TAKE TODAY TO ENSURE THAT YOU REACH YOUR BIG GOAL?

_____

_____

_____

◼ MORNING RITUAL

SUCCESS STARTS IN THE HABITS YOU CREATE FROM THE TIME YOU WAKE UP. HOW WILL YOU PREPARE YOUR MIND FOR ACTION TODAY?

I WILL _____

I WILL _____

I WILL _____

◼ GRATITUDE

PEOPLE WHO PRACTICE THE HABIT OF GRATITUDE ATTRACT MORE SUCCESS. WHO OR WHAT ARE YOU GRATEFUL FOR TODAY?

_____   _____

_____   _____

_____   _____

DAY ____

f FACEBOOK CHECK-IN

COMMENT ON TODAY'S POST IN THE **RE-INVENT 360 JOURNAL COMMUNITY** FACEBOOK GROUP.

■ FITNESS FOCUS

A HEALTHY MIND IN A HEALTHY BODY. WHAT WILL YOU DO TODAY TO STAY ACTIVE?

_____

■ CONNECTING

WHO WILL YOU TALK TO TODAY TO GET YOU ONE STEP CLOSER TOWARDS REACHING YOUR GOAL?

_____

_____

☾ EVENING REFLECTION

■ TODAY'S WINS

NOW THAT THE DAY IS OVER, REFLECT ON WHAT YOU DID TODAY THAT HELPED YOU TO GET CLOSER TO YOUR BIG GOAL

_____   _____

_____   _____

■ PUSHING BEYOND

WHAT CAN YOU DO TOMORRROW TO IMPROVE ON THE LESSONS THAT YOU LEARNED TODAY?

_____

_____

_____

DAY ____

> " *Believe in yourself and all that you are. Know that there is something inside you that is greater than any obstacle.*
> — *Christian Larson*

■ THE BIG GOAL

WHAT WILL YOU ACHIEVE TODAY TO GET YOU ONE STEP CLOSER TO ACHIEVING YOUR DREAM?

_____

_____

■ TAKING ACTION

WHAT STEPS WILL YOU TAKE TODAY TO ENSURE THAT YOU REACH YOUR BIG GOAL?

1 _____

2 _____

3 _____

■ MORNING RITUAL

SUCCESS STARTS IN THE HABITS YOU CREATE FROM THE TIME YOU WAKE UP. HOW WILL YOU PREPARE YOUR MIND FOR ACTION TODAY?

I WILL _____

I WILL _____

I WILL _____

■ GRATITUDE

PEOPLE WHO PRACTICE THE HABIT OF GRATITUDE ATTRACT MORE SUCCESS. WHO OR WHAT ARE YOU GRATEFUL FOR TODAY?

_____   _____

_____   _____

_____   _____

DAY ____

FACEBOOK CHECK-IN

COMMENT ON TODAY'S POST IN THE **RE-INVENT 360 JOURNAL COMMUNITY** FACEBOOK GROUP.

■ FITNESS FOCUS

A HEALTHY MIND IN A HEALTHY BODY. WHAT WILL YOU DO TODAY TO STAY ACTIVE?

_____

■ CONNECTING

WHO WILL YOU TALK TO TODAY TO GET YOU ONE STEP CLOSER TOWARDS REACHING YOUR GOAL?

_____

_____

EVENING REFLECTION

■ TODAY'S WINS

NOW THAT THE DAY IS OVER, REFLECT ON WHAT YOU DID TODAY THAT HELPED YOU TO GET CLOSER TO YOUR BIG GOAL

_____   _____

_____   _____

■ PUSHING BEYOND

WHAT CAN YOU DO TOMORRROW TO IMPROVE ON THE LESSONS THAT YOU LEARNED TODAY?

_____

_____

_____

DAY ____

> ❝ *Believe in your infinite potential. Your only limitations are those you set upon yourself. — Roy T. Bennett*

■ THE BIG GOAL

WHAT WILL YOU ACHIEVE TODAY TO GET YOU ONE STEP CLOSER TO ACHIEVING YOUR DREAM?

_____

_____

■ TAKING ACTION

WHAT STEPS WILL YOU TAKE TODAY TO ENSURE THAT YOU REACH YOUR BIG GOAL?

_____

_____

_____

■ MORNING RITUAL

SUCCESS STARTS IN THE HABITS YOU CREATE FROM THE TIME YOU WAKE UP. HOW WILL YOU PREPARE YOUR MIND FOR ACTION TODAY?

I WILL _____

I WILL _____

I WILL _____

■ GRATITUDE

PEOPLE WHO PRACTICE THE HABIT OF GRATITUDE ATTRACT MORE SUCCESS. WHO OR WHAT ARE YOU GRATEFUL FOR TODAY?

_____   _____

_____   _____

_____   _____

DAY ____

FACEBOOK CHECK-IN

COMMENT ON TODAY'S POST IN THE **RE-INVENT 360 JOURNAL COMMUNITY** FACEBOOK GROUP.

■ FITNESS FOCUS

A HEALTHY MIND IN A HEALTHY BODY. WHAT WILL YOU DO TODAY TO STAY ACTIVE?

_____

■ CONNECTING

WHO WILL YOU TALK TO TODAY TO GET YOU ONE STEP CLOSER TOWARDS REACHING YOUR GOAL?

_____

_____

☾ EVENING REFLECTION

■ TODAY'S WINS

NOW THAT THE DAY IS OVER, REFLECT ON WHAT YOU DID TODAY THAT HELPED YOU TO GET CLOSER TO YOUR BIG GOAL

_____   _____

_____   _____

■ PUSHING BEYOND

WHAT CAN YOU DO TOMORRROW TO IMPROVE ON THE LESSONS THAT YOU LEARNED TODAY?

_____

_____

_____

DAY ___

> *If you want to make a permanent change, stop focusing on the size of your problems and start focusing on the size of you. — T. Harv Eker*

■ THE BIG GOAL

WHAT WILL YOU ACHIEVE TODAY TO GET YOU ONE STEP CLOSER TO ACHIEVING YOUR DREAM?

_____

_____

■ TAKING ACTION

WHAT STEPS WILL YOU TAKE TODAY TO ENSURE THAT YOU REACH YOUR BIG GOAL?

1. _____

2. _____

3. _____

■ MORNING RITUAL

SUCCESS STARTS IN THE HABITS YOU CREATE FROM THE TIME YOU WAKE UP. HOW WILL YOU PREPARE YOUR MIND FOR ACTION TODAY?

I WILL _____

I WILL _____

I WILL _____

■ GRATITUDE

PEOPLE WHO PRACTICE THE HABIT OF GRATITUDE ATTRACT MORE SUCCESS. WHO OR WHAT ARE YOU GRATEFUL FOR TODAY?

_____   _____

_____   _____

_____   _____

DAY ____

 ## FACEBOOK CHECK-IN
COMMENT ON TODAY'S POST IN THE **RE-INVENT 360 JOURNAL COMMUNITY** FACEBOOK GROUP.

■ FITNESS FOCUS
A HEALTHY MIND IN A HEALTHY BODY. WHAT WILL YOU DO TODAY TO STAY ACTIVE?

_____

■ CONNECTING
WHO WILL YOU TALK TO TODAY TO GET YOU ONE STEP CLOSER TOWARDS REACHING YOUR GOAL?

_____

_____

 ## EVENING REFLECTION

■ TODAY'S WINS
NOW THAT THE DAY IS OVER, REFLECT ON WHAT YOU DID TODAY THAT HELPED YOU TO GET CLOSER TO YOUR BIG GOAL

_____   _____

_____   _____

■ PUSHING BEYOND
WHAT CAN YOU DO TOMORRROW TO IMPROVE ON THE LESSONS THAT YOU LEARNED TODAY?

_____

_____

_____

DAY ____

> **"** *If you can't figure out your purpose, figure out your passion. For your passion will lead you right into your purpose. — Bishop T.D. Jakes*

■ THE BIG GOAL

WHAT WILL YOU ACHIEVE TODAY TO GET YOU ONE STEP CLOSER TO ACHIEVING YOUR DREAM?

_____

_____

■ TAKING ACTION

WHAT STEPS WILL YOU TAKE TODAY TO ENSURE THAT YOU REACH YOUR BIG GOAL?

1 _____

2 _____

3 _____

■ MORNING RITUAL

SUCCESS STARTS IN THE HABITS YOU CREATE FROM THE TIME YOU WAKE UP. HOW WILL YOU PREPARE YOUR MIND FOR ACTION TODAY?

I WILL _____

I WILL _____

I WILL _____

■ GRATITUDE

PEOPLE WHO PRACTICE THE HABIT OF GRATITUDE ATTRACT MORE SUCCESS. WHO OR WHAT ARE YOU GRATEFUL FOR TODAY?

_____   _____

_____   _____

_____   _____

DAY ____

FACEBOOK CHECK-IN
COMMENT ON TODAY'S POST IN THE **RE-INVENT 360 JOURNAL COMMUNITY** FACEBOOK GROUP.

■ FITNESS FOCUS
A HEALTHY MIND IN A HEALTHY BODY. WHAT WILL YOU DO TODAY TO STAY ACTIVE?

_____

■ CONNECTING
WHO WILL YOU TALK TO TODAY TO GET YOU ONE STEP CLOSER TOWARDS REACHING YOUR GOAL?

_____

_____

EVENING REFLECTION

■ TODAY'S WINS
NOW THAT THE DAY IS OVER, REFLECT ON WHAT YOU DID TODAY THAT HELPED YOU TO GET CLOSER TO YOUR BIG GOAL

_____   _____

_____   _____

■ PUSHING BEYOND
WHAT CAN YOU DO TOMORRROW TO IMPROVE ON THE LESSONS THAT YOU LEARNED TODAY?

_____

_____

_____

DAY _____

> 66 *Our lives are a sum total of the choices we have made.*
> *— Dr. Wayne Dyer*

◀ THE BIG GOAL

WHAT WILL YOU ACHIEVE TODAY TO GET YOU ONE STEP CLOSER TO ACHIEVING YOUR DREAM?

_____

_____

◀ TAKING ACTION

WHAT STEPS WILL YOU TAKE TODAY TO ENSURE THAT YOU REACH YOUR BIG GOAL?

1 _____

2 _____

3 _____

◀ MORNING RITUAL

SUCCESS STARTS IN THE HABITS YOU CREATE FROM THE TIME YOU WAKE UP. HOW WILL YOU PREPARE YOUR MIND FOR ACTION TODAY?

I WILL _____

I WILL _____

I WILL _____

◀ GRATITUDE

PEOPLE WHO PRACTICE THE HABIT OF GRATITUDE ATTRACT MORE SUCCESS. WHO OR WHAT ARE YOU GRATEFUL FOR TODAY?

_____   _____

_____   _____

_____   _____

DAY ____

FACEBOOK CHECK-IN

COMMENT ON TODAY'S POST IN THE **RE-INVENT 360 JOURNAL COMMUNITY** FACEBOOK GROUP.

■ FITNESS FOCUS

A HEALTHY MIND IN A HEALTHY BODY. WHAT WILL YOU DO TODAY TO STAY ACTIVE?

_____

■ CONNECTING

WHO WILL YOU TALK TO TODAY TO GET YOU ONE STEP CLOSER TOWARDS REACHING YOUR GOAL?

_____

_____

EVENING REFLECTION

■ TODAY'S WINS

NOW THAT THE DAY IS OVER, REFLECT ON WHAT YOU DID TODAY THAT HELPED YOU TO GET CLOSER TO YOUR BIG GOAL

_____   _____

_____   _____

■ PUSHING BEYOND

WHAT CAN YOU DO TOMORRROW TO IMPROVE ON THE LESSONS THAT YOU LEARNED TODAY?

_____

_____

_____

DAY ____

> *One minute of anger weakens your immune system for 4-5 hours. One minute of laughter boosts your immune system for over 24 hours. — Olivia*

■ THE BIG GOAL

WHAT WILL YOU ACHIEVE TODAY TO GET YOU ONE STEP CLOSER TO ACHIEVING YOUR DREAM?

_____

_____

■ TAKING ACTION

WHAT STEPS WILL YOU TAKE TODAY TO ENSURE THAT YOU REACH YOUR BIG GOAL?

1 _____

2 _____

3 _____

■ MORNING RITUAL

SUCCESS STARTS IN THE HABITS YOU CREATE FROM THE TIME YOU WAKE UP. HOW WILL YOU PREPARE YOUR MIND FOR ACTION TODAY?

I WILL _____

I WILL _____

I WILL _____

■ GRATITUDE

PEOPLE WHO PRACTICE THE HABIT OF GRATITUDE ATTRACT MORE SUCCESS. WHO OR WHAT ARE YOU GRATEFUL FOR TODAY?

_____   _____

_____   _____

_____   _____

115

DAY ____

FACEBOOK CHECK-IN
COMMENT ON TODAY'S POST IN THE **RE-INVENT 360 JOURNAL COMMUNITY** FACEBOOK GROUP.

■ FITNESS FOCUS
A HEALTHY MIND IN A HEALTHY BODY. WHAT WILL YOU DO TODAY TO STAY ACTIVE?

_____

■ CONNECTING
WHO WILL YOU TALK TO TODAY TO GET YOU ONE STEP CLOSER TOWARDS REACHING YOUR GOAL?

_____

_____

EVENING REFLECTION

■ TODAY'S WINS
NOW THAT THE DAY IS OVER, REFLECT ON WHAT YOU DID TODAY THAT HELPED YOU TO GET CLOSER TO YOUR BIG GOAL

_____   _____

_____   _____

■ PUSHING BEYOND
WHAT CAN YOU DO TOMORRROW TO IMPROVE ON THE LESSONS THAT YOU LEARNED TODAY?

_____

_____

_____

DAY _____

" *Love yourself first and everything else falls in line. You really have to love yourself to get anything done in this world. — Lucille Ball*

■ THE BIG GOAL

WHAT WILL YOU ACHIEVE TODAY TO GET YOU ONE STEP CLOSER TO ACHIEVING YOUR DREAM?

_____

_____

■ TAKING ACTION

WHAT STEPS WILL YOU TAKE TODAY TO ENSURE THAT YOU REACH YOUR BIG GOAL?

1 _____

2 _____

3 _____

■ MORNING RITUAL

SUCCESS STARTS IN THE HABITS YOU CREATE FROM THE TIME YOU WAKE UP. HOW WILL YOU PREPARE YOUR MIND FOR ACTION TODAY?

I WILL _____

I WILL _____

I WILL _____

■ GRATITUDE

PEOPLE WHO PRACTICE THE HABIT OF GRATITUDE ATTRACT MORE SUCCESS. WHO OR WHAT ARE YOU GRATEFUL FOR TODAY?

_____   _____

_____   _____

_____   _____

DAY ____

FACEBOOK CHECK-IN
COMMENT ON TODAY'S POST IN THE **RE-INVENT 360 JOURNAL COMMUNITY** FACEBOOK GROUP.

■ FITNESS FOCUS
A HEALTHY MIND IN A HEALTHY BODY. WHAT WILL YOU DO TODAY TO STAY ACTIVE?

_____

■ CONNECTING
WHO WILL YOU TALK TO TODAY TO GET YOU ONE STEP CLOSER TOWARDS REACHING YOUR GOAL?

_____

_____

EVENING REFLECTION

■ TODAY'S WINS
NOW THAT THE DAY IS OVER, REFLECT ON WHAT YOU DID TODAY THAT HELPED YOU TO GET CLOSER TO YOUR BIG GOAL

_____   _____

_____   _____

■ PUSHING BEYOND
WHAT CAN YOU DO TOMORRROW TO IMPROVE ON THE LESSONS THAT YOU LEARNED TODAY?

_____

_____

_____

10-DAY
CHECK IN

" "

Your thoughts become your belief.
Your belief becomes your reality.

SHAZ ALIDINA

10-DAY CHECK IN

■ THE BIG GOAL
HOW MUCH CLOSER ARE YOU TO YOUR GOAL?
(1 – NOT MUCH, 5 – MADE AVERAGE PROGRESS, 10 – BIG STEPS)

CIRCLE ONE: 1   2   3   4   5   6   7   8   9   10

HOW HAS YOUR VISION FOR YOUR BIG GOAL EXPANDED THIS WEEK?

_____

_____

_____

■ TAKING ACTION
WHAT ACTIONS DID YOU FEEL GREAT ABOUT THIS WEEK?

_____

_____

_____

■ MORNING RITUAL
HOW MANY DAYS DID YOU PERFORM YOUR MORNING RITUAL?

CIRCLE ONE: 1   2   3   4   5   6   7   8   9   10

WHICH ACTIVITIES SERVED YOU ESPECIALLY WELL?

_____

_____

_____

■ GRATITUDE
WHICH OF YOUR BIG WINS THIS WEEK ARE YOU MOST GRATEFUL FOR?

_____

_____

HOW CAN YOU BUILD ON THIS WIN?

_____

_____

10-DAY CHECK IN

◼ FITNESS

HOW MANY DAYS DID YOU GET ACTIVE DURING THIS CYCLE?

CIRCLE ONE: 1   2   3   4   5   6   7   8   9   10

IF LESS THAN 5, WHAT CHANGES DO YOU NEED TO MAKE TO CREATE TIME FOR YOUR HEALTH?

_____

_____

◼ CONNECTING

HOW MANY CONNECTIONS DID YOU MAKE THIS WEEK?

CIRCLE ONE: 1   2   3   4   5   6   7   8   9   10

WHICH PERSON PROVED TO BE AN INVALUABLE CONNECTION IN GETTING YOU CLOSER TO YOUR BIG GOAL?

_____

WHAT CAN YOU DO TO IN TURN TO BE AN ASSET TO THEM?

_____

_____

◼ MIND DUMP!

SCRIBBLE OUT EVERYTHING THAT'S ON YOUR MIND AS YOU LOOK TOWARDS THE NEXT 10 DAYS. WHAT NEEDS TO BE DONE? WHO NEEDS TO BE CONTACTED? WHAT TOOLS DO YOU NEED? WRITE. DRAW. DOODLE.

READY. SET.
GO!

DAY ____

> ❝ *The tragedy of life is not death, but what we let die inside of us while we live. — Norman Cousins*

■ THE BIG GOAL

WHAT WILL YOU ACHIEVE TODAY TO GET YOU ONE STEP CLOSER TO ACHIEVING YOUR DREAM?

_____

_____

■ TAKING ACTION

WHAT STEPS WILL YOU TAKE TODAY TO ENSURE THAT YOU REACH YOUR BIG GOAL?

1. _____

2. _____

3. _____

■ MORNING RITUAL

SUCCESS STARTS IN THE HABITS YOU CREATE FROM THE TIME YOU WAKE UP. HOW WILL YOU PREPARE YOUR MIND FOR ACTION TODAY?

I WILL _____

I WILL _____

I WILL _____

■ GRATITUDE

PEOPLE WHO PRACTICE THE HABIT OF GRATITUDE ATTRACT MORE SUCCESS. WHO OR WHAT ARE YOU GRATEFUL FOR TODAY?

_____   _____

_____   _____

_____   _____

DAY ____

FACEBOOK CHECK-IN
COMMENT ON TODAY'S POST IN THE **RE-INVENT 360 JOURNAL COMMUNITY** FACEBOOK GROUP.

■ FITNESS FOCUS
A HEALTHY MIND IN A HEALTHY BODY. WHAT WILL YOU DO TODAY TO STAY ACTIVE?

_____

■ CONNECTING
WHO WILL YOU TALK TO TODAY TO GET YOU ONE STEP CLOSER TOWARDS REACHING YOUR GOAL?

_____

_____

◗ EVENING REFLECTION

■ TODAY'S WINS
NOW THAT THE DAY IS OVER, REFLECT ON WHAT YOU DID TODAY THAT HELPED YOU TO GET CLOSER TO YOUR BIG GOAL

_____   _____

_____   _____

■ PUSHING BEYOND
WHAT CAN YOU DO TOMORROW TO IMPROVE ON THE LESSONS THAT YOU LEARNED TODAY?

_____

_____

_____

DAY ____

" *Trust yourself, you know more than you think you do.*
— Benjamin Spock

■ THE BIG GOAL

WHAT WILL YOU ACHIEVE TODAY TO GET YOU ONE STEP CLOSER TO
ACHIEVING YOUR DREAM?

_____

_____

■ TAKING ACTION

WHAT STEPS WILL YOU TAKE TODAY TO ENSURE THAT YOU REACH
YOUR BIG GOAL?

_____

_____

_____

■ MORNING RITUAL

SUCCESS STARTS IN THE HABITS YOU CREATE FROM THE TIME YOU
WAKE UP. HOW WILL YOU PREPARE YOUR MIND FOR ACTION TODAY?

I WILL _____

I WILL _____

I WILL _____

■ GRATITUDE

PEOPLE WHO PRACTICE THE HABIT OF GRATITUDE ATTRACT MORE
SUCCESS. WHO OR WHAT ARE YOU GRATEFUL FOR TODAY?

_____   _____

_____   _____

_____   _____

DAY ____

FACEBOOK CHECK-IN

COMMENT ON TODAY'S POST IN THE **RE-INVENT 360 JOURNAL COMMUNITY** FACEBOOK GROUP.

■ FITNESS FOCUS

A HEALTHY MIND IN A HEALTHY BODY. WHAT WILL YOU DO TODAY TO STAY ACTIVE?

■ CONNECTING

WHO WILL YOU TALK TO TODAY TO GET YOU ONE STEP CLOSER TOWARDS REACHING YOUR GOAL?

EVENING REFLECTION

■ TODAY'S WINS

NOW THAT THE DAY IS OVER, REFLECT ON WHAT YOU DID TODAY THAT HELPED YOU TO GET CLOSER TO YOUR BIG GOAL

■ PUSHING BEYOND

WHAT CAN YOU DO TOMORROW TO IMPROVE ON THE LESSONS THAT YOU LEARNED TODAY?

DAY ____

You can conquer almost any fear if you will only make up your mind to do so. For remember, fear doesn't exist anywhere except in the mind. — *Dale Carnegie*

THE BIG GOAL

WHAT WILL YOU ACHIEVE TODAY TO GET YOU ONE STEP CLOSER TO ACHIEVING YOUR DREAM?

_____

_____

TAKING ACTION

WHAT STEPS WILL YOU TAKE TODAY TO ENSURE THAT YOU REACH YOUR BIG GOAL?

_____

_____

_____

MORNING RITUAL

SUCCESS STARTS IN THE HABITS YOU CREATE FROM THE TIME YOU WAKE UP. HOW WILL YOU PREPARE YOUR MIND FOR ACTION TODAY?

I WILL _____

I WILL _____

I WILL _____

GRATITUDE

PEOPLE WHO PRACTICE THE HABIT OF GRATITUDE ATTRACT MORE SUCCESS. WHO OR WHAT ARE YOU GRATEFUL FOR TODAY?

_____   _____

_____   _____

_____   _____

DAY ____

FACEBOOK CHECK-IN
COMMENT ON TODAY'S POST IN THE **RE-INVENT 360 JOURNAL COMMUNITY** FACEBOOK GROUP.

■ FITNESS FOCUS
A HEALTHY MIND IN A HEALTHY BODY. WHAT WILL YOU DO TODAY TO STAY ACTIVE?

■ CONNECTING
WHO WILL YOU TALK TO TODAY TO GET YOU ONE STEP CLOSER TOWARDS REACHING YOUR GOAL?

☾ EVENING REFLECTION

■ TODAY'S WINS
NOW THAT THE DAY IS OVER, REFLECT ON WHAT YOU DID TODAY THAT HELPED YOU TO GET CLOSER TO YOUR BIG GOAL

■ PUSHING BEYOND
WHAT CAN YOU DO TOMORRROW TO IMPROVE ON THE LESSONS THAT YOU LEARNED TODAY?

DAY ____

> ❝ *It's not what you look at that matters, its what you see.*
> *— Henry David Thoreau*

■ THE BIG GOAL

WHAT WILL YOU ACHIEVE TODAY TO GET YOU ONE STEP CLOSER TO
ACHIEVING YOUR DREAM?

_____

_____

■ TAKING ACTION

WHAT STEPS WILL YOU TAKE TODAY TO ENSURE THAT YOU REACH
YOUR BIG GOAL?

_____

_____

_____

■ MORNING RITUAL

SUCCESS STARTS IN THE HABITS YOU CREATE FROM THE TIME YOU
WAKE UP. HOW WILL YOU PREPARE YOUR MIND FOR ACTION TODAY?

WILL _____

WILL _____

WILL _____

■ GRATITUDE

PEOPLE WHO PRACTICE THE HABIT OF GRATITUDE ATTRACT MORE
SUCCESS. WHO OR WHAT ARE YOU GRATEFUL FOR TODAY?

_____   _____

_____   _____

_____   _____

DAY _____

FACEBOOK CHECK-IN
COMMENT ON TODAY'S POST IN THE **RE-INVENT 360 JOURNAL COMMUNITY** FACEBOOK GROUP.

■ FITNESS FOCUS
A HEALTHY MIND IN A HEALTHY BODY. WHAT WILL YOU DO TODAY TO STAY ACTIVE?

_____

■ CONNECTING
WHO WILL YOU TALK TO TODAY TO GET YOU ONE STEP CLOSER TOWARDS REACHING YOUR GOAL?

_____

_____

EVENING REFLECTION

■ TODAY'S WINS
NOW THAT THE DAY IS OVER, REFLECT ON WHAT YOU DID TODAY THAT HELPED YOU TO GET CLOSER TO YOUR BIG GOAL

_____   _____

_____   _____

■ PUSHING BEYOND
WHAT CAN YOU DO TOMORROW TO IMPROVE ON THE LESSONS THAT YOU LEARNED TODAY?

_____

_____

_____

DAY ____

DATE _____

> " *If your actions inspire others to dream more, learn more,*
> *do more and become more, you are a leader.*
> — *John Quincy Adams*

▪ THE BIG GOAL

WHAT WILL YOU ACHIEVE TODAY TO GET YOU ONE STEP CLOSER TO ACHIEVING YOUR DREAM?

_____

_____

▪ TAKING ACTION

WHAT STEPS WILL YOU TAKE TODAY TO ENSURE THAT YOU REACH YOUR BIG GOAL?

_____

_____

_____

▪ MORNING RITUAL

SUCCESS STARTS IN THE HABITS YOU CREATE FROM THE TIME YOU WAKE UP. HOW WILL YOU PREPARE YOUR MIND FOR ACTION TODAY?

I WILL _____

I WILL _____

I WILL _____

▪ GRATITUDE

PEOPLE WHO PRACTICE THE HABIT OF GRATITUDE ATTRACT MORE SUCCESS. WHO OR WHAT ARE YOU GRATEFUL FOR TODAY?

_____   _____

_____   _____

_____   _____

DAY ___

FACEBOOK CHECK-IN
COMMENT ON TODAY'S POST IN THE **RE-INVENT 360 JOURNAL COMMUNITY** FACEBOOK GROUP.

■ FITNESS FOCUS
A HEALTHY MIND IN A HEALTHY BODY. WHAT WILL YOU DO TODAY TO STAY ACTIVE?

_____

■ CONNECTING
WHO WILL YOU TALK TO TODAY TO GET YOU ONE STEP CLOSER TOWARDS REACHING YOUR GOAL?

_____

_____

(EVENING REFLECTION

■ TODAY'S WINS
NOW THAT THE DAY IS OVER, REFLECT ON WHAT YOU DID TODAY THAT HELPED YOU TO GET CLOSER TO YOUR BIG GOAL

_____   _____

_____   _____

■ PUSHING BEYOND
WHAT CAN YOU DO TOMORRROW TO IMPROVE ON THE LESSONS THAT YOU LEARNED TODAY?

_____

_____

_____

132

DAY ____

DATE _____

> *You alone decide what thoughts and beliefs you let into your life. For they will shape whether you feel rich or poor, cursed or blessed. — Tony Robbins*

■ THE BIG GOAL

WHAT WILL YOU ACHIEVE TODAY TO GET YOU ONE STEP CLOSER TO ACHIEVING YOUR DREAM?

_____

_____

■ TAKING ACTION

WHAT STEPS WILL YOU TAKE TODAY TO ENSURE THAT YOU REACH YOUR BIG GOAL?

_____

_____

_____

■ MORNING RITUAL

SUCCESS STARTS IN THE HABITS YOU CREATE FROM THE TIME YOU WAKE UP. HOW WILL YOU PREPARE YOUR MIND FOR ACTION TODAY?

I WILL _____

I WILL _____

I WILL _____

■ GRATITUDE

PEOPLE WHO PRACTICE THE HABIT OF GRATITUDE ATTRACT MORE SUCCESS. WHO OR WHAT ARE YOU GRATEFUL FOR TODAY?

_____   _____

_____   _____

_____   _____

DAY ____

FACEBOOK CHECK-IN
COMMENT ON TODAY'S POST IN THE **RE-INVENT 360 JOURNAL COMMUNITY** FACEBOOK GROUP.

■ FITNESS FOCUS
A HEALTHY MIND IN A HEALTHY BODY. WHAT WILL YOU DO TODAY TO STAY ACTIVE?

_____

■ CONNECTING
WHO WILL YOU TALK TO TODAY TO GET YOU ONE STEP CLOSER TOWARDS REACHING YOUR GOAL?

_____

_____

☾ EVENING REFLECTION

■ TODAY'S WINS
NOW THAT THE DAY IS OVER, REFLECT ON WHAT YOU DID TODAY THAT HELPED YOU TO GET CLOSER TO YOUR BIG GOAL

_____   _____

_____   _____

■ PUSHING BEYOND
WHAT CAN YOU DO TOMORRROW TO IMPROVE ON THE LESSONS THAT YOU LEARNED TODAY?

_____

_____

_____

DAY ____

DATE _____

> ❝ *The greater the obstacle, the more glory in overcoming it.*
> *— Moliere*

◀ THE BIG GOAL

WHAT WILL YOU ACHIEVE TODAY TO GET YOU ONE STEP CLOSER TO ACHIEVING YOUR DREAM?

_____

_____

◀ TAKING ACTION

WHAT STEPS WILL YOU TAKE TODAY TO ENSURE THAT YOU REACH YOUR BIG GOAL?

_____

_____

_____

◀ MORNING RITUAL

SUCCESS STARTS IN THE HABITS YOU CREATE FROM THE TIME YOU WAKE UP. HOW WILL YOU PREPARE YOUR MIND FOR ACTION TODAY?

I WILL _____

I WILL _____

I WILL _____

◀ GRATITUDE

PEOPLE WHO PRACTICE THE HABIT OF GRATITUDE ATTRACT MORE SUCCESS. WHO OR WHAT ARE YOU GRATEFUL FOR TODAY?

_____   _____

_____   _____

_____   _____

135

FACEBOOK CHECK-IN

COMMENT ON TODAY'S POST IN THE **RE-INVENT 360 JOURNAL COMMUNITY** FACEBOOK GROUP.

■ FITNESS FOCUS

A HEALTHY MIND IN A HEALTHY BODY. WHAT WILL YOU DO TODAY TO STAY ACTIVE?

■ CONNECTING

WHO WILL YOU TALK TO TODAY TO GET YOU ONE STEP CLOSER TOWARDS REACHING YOUR GOAL?

EVENING REFLECTION

■ TODAY'S WINS

NOW THAT THE DAY IS OVER, REFLECT ON WHAT YOU DID TODAY THAT HELPED YOU TO GET CLOSER TO YOUR BIG GOAL

■ PUSHING BEYOND

WHAT CAN YOU DO TOMORRROW TO IMPROVE ON THE LESSONS THAT YOU LEARNED TODAY?

DAY ____

DATE _____

> *Don't gain the world and lose your soul, wisdom is better than silver and gold. — Bob Marley*

■ THE BIG GOAL

WHAT WILL YOU ACHIEVE TODAY TO GET YOU ONE STEP CLOSER TO ACHIEVING YOUR DREAM?

_____

_____

■ TAKING ACTION

WHAT STEPS WILL YOU TAKE TODAY TO ENSURE THAT YOU REACH YOUR BIG GOAL?

1 _____

2 _____

3 _____

■ MORNING RITUAL

SUCCESS STARTS IN THE HABITS YOU CREATE FROM THE TIME YOU WAKE UP. HOW WILL YOU PREPARE YOUR MIND FOR ACTION TODAY?

I WILL _____

I WILL _____

I WILL _____

■ GRATITUDE

PEOPLE WHO PRACTICE THE HABIT OF GRATITUDE ATTRACT MORE SUCCESS. WHO OR WHAT ARE YOU GRATEFUL FOR TODAY?

_____   _____

_____   _____

_____   _____

DAY ____

FACEBOOK CHECK-IN

COMMENT ON TODAY'S POST IN THE **RE-INVENT 360 JOURNAL COMMUNITY** FACEBOOK GROUP.

◼ FITNESS FOCUS

A HEALTHY MIND IN A HEALTHY BODY. WHAT WILL YOU DO TODAY TO STAY ACTIVE?

_____

◼ CONNECTING

WHO WILL YOU TALK TO TODAY TO GET YOU ONE STEP CLOSER TOWARDS REACHING YOUR GOAL?

_____

_____

EVENING REFLECTION

◼ TODAY'S WINS

NOW THAT THE DAY IS OVER, REFLECT ON WHAT YOU DID TODAY THAT HELPED YOU TO GET CLOSER TO YOUR BIG GOAL

_____   _____

_____   _____

◼ PUSHING BEYOND

WHAT CAN YOU DO TOMORRROW TO IMPROVE ON THE LESSONS THAT YOU LEARNED TODAY?

_____

_____

_____

_____

DAY ____

> " *Your only limitations are those you set up in your mind, or permit others to set up for you. — Og Mandino*

◼ THE BIG GOAL

WHAT WILL YOU ACHIEVE TODAY TO GET YOU ONE STEP CLOSER TO ACHIEVING YOUR DREAM?

_____

_____

◼ TAKING ACTION

WHAT STEPS WILL YOU TAKE TODAY TO ENSURE THAT YOU REACH YOUR BIG GOAL?

_____

_____

_____

◼ MORNING RITUAL

SUCCESS STARTS IN THE HABITS YOU CREATE FROM THE TIME YOU WAKE UP. HOW WILL YOU PREPARE YOUR MIND FOR ACTION TODAY?

I WILL _____

I WILL _____

I WILL _____

◼ GRATITUDE

PEOPLE WHO PRACTICE THE HABIT OF GRATITUDE ATTRACT MORE SUCCESS. WHO OR WHAT ARE YOU GRATEFUL FOR TODAY?

_____   _____

_____   _____

_____   _____

FACEBOOK CHECK-IN

COMMENT ON TODAY'S POST IN THE **RE-INVENT 360 JOURNAL COMMUNITY** FACEBOOK GROUP.

■ FITNESS FOCUS

A HEALTHY MIND IN A HEALTHY BODY. WHAT WILL YOU DO TODAY TO STAY ACTIVE?

_____

■ CONNECTING

WHO WILL YOU TALK TO TODAY TO GET YOU ONE STEP CLOSER TOWARDS REACHING YOUR GOAL?

_____

_____

EVENING REFLECTION

■ TODAY'S WINS

NOW THAT THE DAY IS OVER, REFLECT ON WHAT YOU DID TODAY THAT HELPED YOU TO GET CLOSER TO YOUR BIG GOAL

_____   _____

_____   _____

■ PUSHING BEYOND

WHAT CAN YOU DO TOMORRROW TO IMPROVE ON THE LESSONS THAT YOU LEARNED TODAY?

_____

_____

_____

DAY ____

Move to gratitude when you encounter your frustrations.
And see every event as an opportunity.
— Neale Donald Walsch

■ THE BIG GOAL

WHAT WILL YOU ACHIEVE TODAY TO GET YOU ONE STEP CLOSER TO
ACHIEVING YOUR DREAM?

_____

_____

■ TAKING ACTION

WHAT STEPS WILL YOU TAKE TODAY TO ENSURE THAT YOU REACH
YOUR BIG GOAL?

1 _____

2 _____

3 _____

■ MORNING RITUAL

SUCCESS STARTS IN THE HABITS YOU CREATE FROM THE TIME YOU
WAKE UP. HOW WILL YOU PREPARE YOUR MIND FOR ACTION TODAY?

I WILL _____

I WILL _____

I WILL _____

■ GRATITUDE

PEOPLE WHO PRACTICE THE HABIT OF GRATITUDE ATTRACT MORE
SUCCESS. WHO OR WHAT ARE YOU GRATEFUL FOR TODAY?

_____   _____

_____   _____

_____   _____

DAY ____

FACEBOOK CHECK-IN

COMMENT ON TODAY'S POST IN THE **RE-INVENT 360 JOURNAL COMMUNITY** FACEBOOK GROUP.

■ FITNESS FOCUS

A HEALTHY MIND IN A HEALTHY BODY. WHAT WILL YOU DO TODAY TO STAY ACTIVE?

_____

■ CONNECTING

WHO WILL YOU TALK TO TODAY TO GET YOU ONE STEP CLOSER TOWARDS REACHING YOUR GOAL?

_____

_____

EVENING REFLECTION

■ TODAY'S WINS

NOW THAT THE DAY IS OVER, REFLECT ON WHAT YOU DID TODAY THAT HELPED YOU TO GET CLOSER TO YOUR BIG GOAL

_____   _____

_____   _____

■ PUSHING BEYOND

WHAT CAN YOU DO TOMORRROW TO IMPROVE ON THE LESSONS THAT YOU LEARNED TODAY?

_____

_____

_____

10-DAY
CHECK IN

" "

When you feel torn between two paths...
pick the one that excites you the most.

SHAZ ALIDINA

10-DAY CHECK IN

■ THE BIG GOAL
HOW MUCH CLOSER ARE YOU TO YOUR GOAL?
(1 – NOT MUCH, 5 – MADE AVERAGE PROGRESS, 10 – BIG STEPS)

CIRCLE ONE: 1   2   3   4   5   6   7   8   9   10

HOW HAS YOUR VISION FOR YOUR BIG GOAL EXPANDED THIS WEEK?

_____

_____

_____

■ TAKING ACTION
WHAT ACTIONS DID YOU FEEL GREAT ABOUT THIS WEEK?

_____

_____

_____

■ MORNING RITUAL
HOW MANY DAYS DID YOU PERFORM YOUR MORNING RITUAL?

CIRCLE ONE: 1   2   3   4   5   6   7   8   9   10

WHICH ACTIVITIES SERVED YOU ESPECIALLY WELL?

_____

_____

_____

■ GRATITUDE
WHICH OF YOUR BIG WINS THIS WEEK ARE YOU MOST GRATEFUL FOR?

_____

_____

HOW CAN YOU BUILD ON THIS WIN?

_____

_____

_____

10-DAY CHECK IN

■ FITNESS

HOW MANY DAYS DID YOU GET ACTIVE DURING THIS CYCLE?

CIRCLE ONE: 1   2   3   4   5   6   7   8   9   10

IF LESS THAN 5, WHAT CHANGES DO YOU NEED TO MAKE TO CREATE TIME FOR YOUR HEALTH?

_____

_____

■ CONNECTING

HOW MANY CONNECTIONS DID YOU MAKE THIS WEEK?

CIRCLE ONE: 1   2   3   4   5   6   7   8   9   10

WHICH PERSON PROVED TO BE AN INVALUABLE CONNECTION IN GETTING YOU CLOSER TO YOUR BIG GOAL?

_____

WHAT CAN YOU DO TO IN TURN TO BE AN ASSET TO THEM?

_____

_____

■ MIND DUMP!

SCRIBBLE OUT EVERYTHING THAT'S ON YOUR MIND AS YOU LOOK TOWARDS THE NEXT 10 DAYS. WHAT NEEDS TO BE DONE? WHO NEEDS TO BE CONTACTED? WHAT TOOLS DO YOU NEED? WRITE. DRAW. DOODLE.

READY. SET.
GO!

DAY ____

> ❝ *Talking about our problems is our greatest addiction.*
> *Break the habit. Talk about your joys. — Rita Schiano*

■ THE BIG GOAL

WHAT WILL YOU ACHIEVE TODAY TO GET YOU ONE STEP CLOSER TO
ACHIEVING YOUR DREAM?

_____

_____

■ TAKING ACTION

WHAT STEPS WILL YOU TAKE TODAY TO ENSURE THAT YOU REACH
YOUR BIG GOAL?

1 _____

2 _____

3 _____

■ MORNING RITUAL

SUCCESS STARTS IN THE HABITS YOU CREATE FROM THE TIME YOU
WAKE UP. HOW WILL YOU PREPARE YOUR MIND FOR ACTION TODAY?

I WILL _____

I WILL _____

I WILL _____

■ GRATITUDE

PEOPLE WHO PRACTICE THE HABIT OF GRATITUDE ATTRACT MORE
SUCCESS. WHO OR WHAT ARE YOU GRATEFUL FOR TODAY?

_____   _____

_____   _____

_____   _____

DAY _____

FACEBOOK CHECK-IN
COMMENT ON TODAY'S POST IN THE **RE-INVENT 360 JOURNAL COMMUNITY** FACEBOOK GROUP.

■ FITNESS FOCUS
A HEALTHY MIND IN A HEALTHY BODY. WHAT WILL YOU DO TODAY TO STAY ACTIVE?

_____

■ CONNECTING
WHO WILL YOU TALK TO TODAY TO GET YOU ONE STEP CLOSER TOWARDS REACHING YOUR GOAL?

_____

_____

EVENING REFLECTION

■ TODAY'S WINS
NOW THAT THE DAY IS OVER, REFLECT ON WHAT YOU DID TODAY THAT HELPED YOU TO GET CLOSER TO YOUR BIG GOAL

_____   _____

_____   _____

■ PUSHING BEYOND
WHAT CAN YOU DO TOMORRROW TO IMPROVE ON THE LESSONS THAT YOU LEARNED TODAY?

_____

_____

_____

DAY ____

> ❝ *Perfection is not attainable, but if we chase perfection we can catch excellence.* — *Vince Lombardi*

■ THE BIG GOAL

WHAT WILL YOU ACHIEVE TODAY TO GET YOU ONE STEP CLOSER TO ACHIEVING YOUR DREAM?

_____

_____

■ TAKING ACTION

WHAT STEPS WILL YOU TAKE TODAY TO ENSURE THAT YOU REACH YOUR BIG GOAL?

1 _____

2 _____

3 _____

■ MORNING RITUAL

SUCCESS STARTS IN THE HABITS YOU CREATE FROM THE TIME YOU WAKE UP. HOW WILL YOU PREPARE YOUR MIND FOR ACTION TODAY?

I WILL _____

I WILL _____

I WILL _____

■ GRATITUDE

PEOPLE WHO PRACTICE THE HABIT OF GRATITUDE ATTRACT MORE SUCCESS. WHO OR WHAT ARE YOU GRATEFUL FOR TODAY?

_____   _____

_____   _____

_____   _____

DAY ____

 FACEBOOK CHECK-IN
COMMENT ON TODAY'S POST IN THE **RE-INVENT 360 JOURNAL COMMUNITY** FACEBOOK GROUP.

■ FITNESS FOCUS
A HEALTHY MIND IN A HEALTHY BODY. WHAT WILL YOU DO TODAY TO STAY ACTIVE?

_____

■ CONNECTING
WHO WILL YOU TALK TO TODAY TO GET YOU ONE STEP CLOSER TOWARDS REACHING YOUR GOAL?

_____

_____

 # EVENING REFLECTION

■ TODAY'S WINS
NOW THAT THE DAY IS OVER, REFLECT ON WHAT YOU DID TODAY THAT HELPED YOU TO GET CLOSER TO YOUR BIG GOAL

_____   _____

_____   _____

■ PUSHING BEYOND
WHAT CAN YOU DO TOMORRROW TO IMPROVE ON THE LESSONS THAT YOU LEARNED TODAY?

_____

_____

_____

DAY ____

DATE _____

> 66 *The warrior who trusts his path doesn't need to prove the other is wrong. — Paulo Coelho*

THE BIG GOAL

WHAT WILL YOU ACHIEVE TODAY TO GET YOU ONE STEP CLOSER TO ACHIEVING YOUR DREAM?

_____

_____

TAKING ACTION

WHAT STEPS WILL YOU TAKE TODAY TO ENSURE THAT YOU REACH YOUR BIG GOAL?

_____

_____

_____

MORNING RITUAL

SUCCESS STARTS IN THE HABITS YOU CREATE FROM THE TIME YOU WAKE UP. HOW WILL YOU PREPARE YOUR MIND FOR ACTION TODAY?

WILL _____

WILL _____

WILL _____

GRATITUDE

PEOPLE WHO PRACTICE THE HABIT OF GRATITUDE ATTRACT MORE SUCCESS. WHO OR WHAT ARE YOU GRATEFUL FOR TODAY?

_____   _____

_____   _____

_____   _____

DAY ____

FACEBOOK CHECK-IN
COMMENT ON TODAY'S POST IN THE **RE-INVENT 360 JOURNAL COMMUNITY** FACEBOOK GROUP.

■ FITNESS FOCUS
A HEALTHY MIND IN A HEALTHY BODY. WHAT WILL YOU DO TODAY TO STAY ACTIVE?

■ CONNECTING
WHO WILL YOU TALK TO TODAY TO GET YOU ONE STEP CLOSER TOWARDS REACHING YOUR GOAL?

EVENING REFLECTION

■ TODAY'S WINS
NOW THAT THE DAY IS OVER, REFLECT ON WHAT YOU DID TODAY THAT HELPED YOU TO GET CLOSER TO YOUR BIG GOAL

■ PUSHING BEYOND
WHAT CAN YOU DO TOMORROW TO IMPROVE ON THE LESSONS THAT YOU LEARNED TODAY?

DAY ____

DATE _____

" *Be yourself; everyone else is already taken.*
— Oscar Wilde

■ THE BIG GOAL

WHAT WILL YOU ACHIEVE TODAY TO GET YOU ONE STEP CLOSER TO
ACHIEVING YOUR DREAM?

_____

_____

■ TAKING ACTION

WHAT STEPS WILL YOU TAKE TODAY TO ENSURE THAT YOU REACH
YOUR BIG GOAL?

_____

_____

_____

■ MORNING RITUAL

SUCCESS STARTS IN THE HABITS YOU CREATE FROM THE TIME YOU
WAKE UP. HOW WILL YOU PREPARE YOUR MIND FOR ACTION TODAY?

I WILL _____

I WILL _____

I WILL _____

■ GRATITUDE

PEOPLE WHO PRACTICE THE HABIT OF GRATITUDE ATTRACT MORE
SUCCESS. WHO OR WHAT ARE YOU GRATEFUL FOR TODAY?

_____   _____

_____   _____

_____   _____

DAY ____

FACEBOOK CHECK-IN
COMMENT ON TODAY'S POST IN THE **RE-INVENT 360 JOURNAL COMMUNITY** FACEBOOK GROUP.

■ FITNESS FOCUS
A HEALTHY MIND IN A HEALTHY BODY. WHAT WILL YOU DO TODAY TO STAY ACTIVE?

_____

■ CONNECTING
WHO WILL YOU TALK TO TODAY TO GET YOU ONE STEP CLOSER TOWARDS REACHING YOUR GOAL?

_____

_____

EVENING REFLECTION

■ TODAY'S WINS
NOW THAT THE DAY IS OVER, REFLECT ON WHAT YOU DID TODAY THAT HELPED YOU TO GET CLOSER TO YOUR BIG GOAL

_____   _____

_____   _____

■ PUSHING BEYOND
WHAT CAN YOU DO TOMORRROW TO IMPROVE ON THE LESSONS THAT YOU LEARNED TODAY?

_____

_____

_____

DAY _____

DATE _____

❝ *Life opens up opportunities to you, and you either take them or you stay afraid of taking them.* — *Jim Carrey*

■ THE BIG GOAL

WHAT WILL YOU ACHIEVE TODAY TO GET YOU ONE STEP CLOSER TO ACHIEVING YOUR DREAM?

_____

_____

■ TAKING ACTION

WHAT STEPS WILL YOU TAKE TODAY TO ENSURE THAT YOU REACH YOUR BIG GOAL?

_____

_____

_____

■ MORNING RITUAL

SUCCESS STARTS IN THE HABITS YOU CREATE FROM THE TIME YOU WAKE UP. HOW WILL YOU PREPARE YOUR MIND FOR ACTION TODAY?

I WILL _____

I WILL _____

I WILL _____

■ GRATITUDE

PEOPLE WHO PRACTICE THE HABIT OF GRATITUDE ATTRACT MORE SUCCESS. WHO OR WHAT ARE YOU GRATEFUL FOR TODAY?

_____   _____

_____   _____

_____   _____

FACEBOOK CHECK-IN

COMMENT ON TODAY'S POST IN THE **RE-INVENT 360 JOURNAL COMMUNITY** FACEBOOK GROUP.

■ FITNESS FOCUS

A HEALTHY MIND IN A HEALTHY BODY. WHAT WILL YOU DO TODAY TO STAY ACTIVE?

_____

■ CONNECTING

WHO WILL YOU TALK TO TODAY TO GET YOU ONE STEP CLOSER TOWARDS REACHING YOUR GOAL?

_____

_____

EVENING REFLECTION

■ TODAY'S WINS

NOW THAT THE DAY IS OVER, REFLECT ON WHAT YOU DID TODAY THAT HELPED YOU TO GET CLOSER TO YOUR BIG GOAL

_____   _____

_____   _____

■ PUSHING BEYOND

WHAT CAN YOU DO TOMORRROW TO IMPROVE ON THE LESSONS THAT YOU LEARNED TODAY?

_____

_____

_____

DAY _____

> **"** *Always ask yourself the question "Is this going to help get me to my goal or not? — Bob Proctor*

◼ THE BIG GOAL

WHAT WILL YOU ACHIEVE TODAY TO GET YOU ONE STEP CLOSER TO ACHIEVING YOUR DREAM?

_____

_____

◼ TAKING ACTION

WHAT STEPS WILL YOU TAKE TODAY TO ENSURE THAT YOU REACH YOUR BIG GOAL?

_____

_____

_____

◼ MORNING RITUAL

SUCCESS STARTS IN THE HABITS YOU CREATE FROM THE TIME YOU WAKE UP. HOW WILL YOU PREPARE YOUR MIND FOR ACTION TODAY?

WILL _____

WILL _____

WILL _____

◼ GRATITUDE

PEOPLE WHO PRACTICE THE HABIT OF GRATITUDE ATTRACT MORE SUCCESS. WHO OR WHAT ARE YOU GRATEFUL FOR TODAY?

_____   _____

_____   _____

_____   _____

DAY ____

FACEBOOK CHECK-IN
COMMENT ON TODAY'S POST IN THE **RE-INVENT 360 JOURNAL COMMUNITY** FACEBOOK GROUP.

■ FITNESS FOCUS
A HEALTHY MIND IN A HEALTHY BODY. WHAT WILL YOU DO TODAY TO STAY ACTIVE?

_____

■ CONNECTING
WHO WILL YOU TALK TO TODAY TO GET YOU ONE STEP CLOSER TOWARDS REACHING YOUR GOAL?

_____

_____

☾ EVENING REFLECTION

■ TODAY'S WINS
NOW THAT THE DAY IS OVER, REFLECT ON WHAT YOU DID TODAY THAT HELPED YOU TO GET CLOSER TO YOUR BIG GOAL

_____   _____

_____   _____

■ PUSHING BEYOND
WHAT CAN YOU DO TOMORRROW TO IMPROVE ON THE LESSONS THAT YOU LEARNED TODAY?

_____

_____

_____

DAY ____

> 66 *You must find the place inside yourself where nothing is impossible. — Deepak Chopra*

■ THE BIG GOAL

WHAT WILL YOU ACHIEVE TODAY TO GET YOU ONE STEP CLOSER TO ACHIEVING YOUR DREAM?

_____

_____

■ TAKING ACTION

WHAT STEPS WILL YOU TAKE TODAY TO ENSURE THAT YOU REACH YOUR BIG GOAL?

_____

_____

_____

■ MORNING RITUAL

SUCCESS STARTS IN THE HABITS YOU CREATE FROM THE TIME YOU WAKE UP. HOW WILL YOU PREPARE YOUR MIND FOR ACTION TODAY?

WILL _____

WILL _____

WILL _____

■ GRATITUDE

PEOPLE WHO PRACTICE THE HABIT OF GRATITUDE ATTRACT MORE SUCCESS. WHO OR WHAT ARE YOU GRATEFUL FOR TODAY?

_____   _____

_____   _____

_____   _____

FACEBOOK CHECK-IN

COMMENT ON TODAY'S POST IN THE **RE-INVENT 360 JOURNAL COMMUNITY** FACEBOOK GROUP.

■ FITNESS FOCUS

A HEALTHY MIND IN A HEALTHY BODY. WHAT WILL YOU DO TODAY TO STAY ACTIVE?

_____

■ CONNECTING

WHO WILL YOU TALK TO TODAY TO GET YOU ONE STEP CLOSER TOWARDS REACHING YOUR GOAL?

_____

_____

EVENING REFLECTION

■ TODAY'S WINS

NOW THAT THE DAY IS OVER, REFLECT ON WHAT YOU DID TODAY THAT HELPED YOU TO GET CLOSER TO YOUR BIG GOAL

_____   _____

_____   _____

■ PUSHING BEYOND

WHAT CAN YOU DO TOMORROW TO IMPROVE ON THE LESSONS THAT YOU LEARNED TODAY?

_____

_____

_____

DAY ____

DATE _____

> *When you focus on problems, you will have more problems. When you focus on possibilities, you will have more opportunities. — Zig Zaglar*

THE BIG GOAL

WHAT WILL YOU ACHIEVE TODAY TO GET YOU ONE STEP CLOSER TO ACHIEVING YOUR DREAM?

_____

_____

TAKING ACTION

WHAT STEPS WILL YOU TAKE TODAY TO ENSURE THAT YOU REACH YOUR BIG GOAL?

_____

_____

_____

MORNING RITUAL

SUCCESS STARTS IN THE HABITS YOU CREATE FROM THE TIME YOU WAKE UP. HOW WILL YOU PREPARE YOUR MIND FOR ACTION TODAY?

WILL _____

WILL _____

WILL _____

GRATITUDE

PEOPLE WHO PRACTICE THE HABIT OF GRATITUDE ATTRACT MORE SUCCESS. WHO OR WHAT ARE YOU GRATEFUL FOR TODAY?

_____   _____

_____   _____

_____   _____

DAY ____

 ## FACEBOOK CHECK-IN
COMMENT ON TODAY'S POST IN THE **RE-INVENT 360 JOURNAL COMMUNITY** FACEBOOK GROUP.

■ FITNESS FOCUS
A HEALTHY MIND IN A HEALTHY BODY. WHAT WILL YOU DO TODAY TO STAY ACTIVE?

■ CONNECTING
WHO WILL YOU TALK TO TODAY TO GET YOU ONE STEP CLOSER TOWARDS REACHING YOUR GOAL?

 # EVENING REFLECTION

■ TODAY'S WINS
NOW THAT THE DAY IS OVER, REFLECT ON WHAT YOU DID TODAY THAT HELPED YOU TO GET CLOSER TO YOUR BIG GOAL

■ PUSHING BEYOND
WHAT CAN YOU DO TOMORRROW TO IMPROVE ON THE LESSONS THAT YOU LEARNED TODAY?

DAY ____

DATE _____

> ❝ *The world can only see us as we see ourselves.*
> *— David R. Hawkins*

■ THE BIG GOAL

WHAT WILL YOU ACHIEVE TODAY TO GET YOU ONE STEP CLOSER TO ACHIEVING YOUR DREAM?

_____

_____

■ TAKING ACTION

WHAT STEPS WILL YOU TAKE TODAY TO ENSURE THAT YOU REACH YOUR BIG GOAL?

_____

_____

_____

■ MORNING RITUAL

SUCCESS STARTS IN THE HABITS YOU CREATE FROM THE TIME YOU WAKE UP. HOW WILL YOU PREPARE YOUR MIND FOR ACTION TODAY?

I WILL _____

I WILL _____

I WILL _____

■ GRATITUDE

PEOPLE WHO PRACTICE THE HABIT OF GRATITUDE ATTRACT MORE SUCCESS. WHO OR WHAT ARE YOU GRATEFUL FOR TODAY?

_____   _____

_____   _____

_____   _____

DAY ____

 ## FACEBOOK CHECK-IN
COMMENT ON TODAY'S POST IN THE **RE-INVENT 360 JOURNAL COMMUNITY** FACEBOOK GROUP.

■ FITNESS FOCUS
A HEALTHY MIND IN A HEALTHY BODY. WHAT WILL YOU DO TODAY TO STAY ACTIVE?

_____

■ CONNECTING
WHO WILL YOU TALK TO TODAY TO GET YOU ONE STEP CLOSER TOWARDS REACHING YOUR GOAL?

_____

_____

 # EVENING REFLECTION

■ TODAY'S WINS
NOW THAT THE DAY IS OVER, REFLECT ON WHAT YOU DID TODAY THAT HELPED YOU TO GET CLOSER TO YOUR BIG GOAL

_____   _____

_____   _____

■ PUSHING BEYOND
WHAT CAN YOU DO TOMORROW TO IMPROVE ON THE LESSONS THAT YOU LEARNED TODAY?

_____

_____

_____

DAY ____

❝ *You are an aperture through which the universe is looking at and exploring itself.* — *Alan Watts*

■ THE BIG GOAL

WHAT WILL YOU ACHIEVE TODAY TO GET YOU ONE STEP CLOSER TO ACHIEVING YOUR DREAM?

_____

_____

■ TAKING ACTION

WHAT STEPS WILL YOU TAKE TODAY TO ENSURE THAT YOU REACH YOUR BIG GOAL?

_____

_____

_____

■ MORNING RITUAL

SUCCESS STARTS IN THE HABITS YOU CREATE FROM THE TIME YOU WAKE UP. HOW WILL YOU PREPARE YOUR MIND FOR ACTION TODAY?

WILL _____

WILL _____

WILL _____

■ GRATITUDE

PEOPLE WHO PRACTICE THE HABIT OF GRATITUDE ATTRACT MORE SUCCESS. WHO OR WHAT ARE YOU GRATEFUL FOR TODAY?

_____   _____

_____   _____

_____   _____

DAY ____

FACEBOOK CHECK-IN

COMMENT ON TODAY'S POST IN THE **RE-INVENT 360 JOURNAL COMMUNITY** FACEBOOK GROUP.

■ FITNESS FOCUS

A HEALTHY MIND IN A HEALTHY BODY. WHAT WILL YOU DO TODAY TO STAY ACTIVE?

_____

■ CONNECTING

WHO WILL YOU TALK TO TODAY TO GET YOU ONE STEP CLOSER TOWARDS REACHING YOUR GOAL?

_____

_____

EVENING REFLECTION

■ TODAY'S WINS

NOW THAT THE DAY IS OVER, REFLECT ON WHAT YOU DID TODAY THAT HELPED YOU TO GET CLOSER TO YOUR BIG GOAL

_____   _____

_____   _____

■ PUSHING BEYOND

WHAT CAN YOU DO TOMORRROW TO IMPROVE ON THE LESSONS THAT YOU LEARNED TODAY?

_____

_____

_____

10-DAY
CHECK IN

" "

I first created a vision in my mind, everyday i kept adding the fine details to it... the color, texture, fragrance, feel and when i opened my eyes I remembered that I am here to create reality and not to face one.

SHAZ ALIDINA

10-DAY CHECK IN

■ THE BIG GOAL
HOW MUCH CLOSER ARE YOU TO YOUR GOAL?
(1 - NOT MUCH, 5 - MADE AVERAGE PROGRESS, 10 - BIG STEPS)

CIRCLE ONE: 1   2   3   4   5   6   7   8   9   10

HOW HAS YOUR VISION FOR YOUR BIG GOAL EXPANDED THIS WEEK?
_____
_____
_____

■ TAKING ACTION
WHAT ACTIONS DID YOU FEEL GREAT ABOUT THIS WEEK?
_____
_____
_____

■ MORNING RITUAL
HOW MANY DAYS DID YOU PERFORM YOUR MORNING RITUAL?

CIRCLE ONE: 1   2   3   4   5   6   7   8   9   10

WHICH ACTIVITIES SERVED YOU ESPECIALLY WELL?
_____
_____
_____

■ GRATITUDE
WHICH OF YOUR BIG WINS THIS WEEK ARE YOU MOST GRATEFUL FOR?
_____
_____

HOW CAN YOU BUILD ON THIS WIN?
_____
_____

10-DAY CHECK IN

■ FITNESS
HOW MANY DAYS DID YOU GET ACTIVE DURING THIS CYCLE?

CIRCLE ONE: 1   2   3   4   5   6   7   8   9   10

IF LESS THAN 5, WHAT CHANGES DO YOU NEED TO MAKE TO CREATE TIME FOR YOUR HEALTH?

_____

_____

■ CONNECTING
HOW MANY CONNECTIONS DID YOU MAKE THIS WEEK?

CIRCLE ONE: 1   2   3   4   5   6   7   8   9   10

WHICH PERSON PROVED TO BE AN INVALUABLE CONNECTION IN GETTING YOU CLOSER TO YOUR BIG GOAL?

_____

WHAT CAN YOU DO TO IN TURN TO BE AN ASSET TO THEM?

_____

_____

■ MIND DUMP!
SCRIBBLE OUT EVERYTHING THAT'S ON YOUR MIND AS YOU LOOK TOWARDS THE NEXT 10 DAYS. WHAT NEEDS TO BE DONE? WHO NEEDS TO BE CONTACTED? WHAT TOOLS DO YOU NEED? WRITE. DRAW. DOODLE.

READY. SET.
GO!

DAY ____

> ❝ *Working hard for something we don't care about is called stress; working hard for something we love is called passion. — Simon Sinek*

■ THE BIG GOAL

WHAT WILL YOU ACHIEVE TODAY TO GET YOU ONE STEP CLOSER TO ACHIEVING YOUR DREAM?

_____

_____

■ TAKING ACTION

WHAT STEPS WILL YOU TAKE TODAY TO ENSURE THAT YOU REACH YOUR BIG GOAL?

1 _____

2 _____

3 _____

■ MORNING RITUAL

SUCCESS STARTS IN THE HABITS YOU CREATE FROM THE TIME YOU WAKE UP. HOW WILL YOU PREPARE YOUR MIND FOR ACTION TODAY?

I WILL _____

I WILL _____

I WILL _____

■ GRATITUDE

PEOPLE WHO PRACTICE THE HABIT OF GRATITUDE ATTRACT MORE SUCCESS. WHO OR WHAT ARE YOU GRATEFUL FOR TODAY?

_____   _____

_____   _____

_____   _____

DAY ____

FACEBOOK CHECK-IN
COMMENT ON TODAY'S POST IN THE **RE-INVENT 360 JOURNAL COMMUNITY** FACEBOOK GROUP.

◼ FITNESS FOCUS
A HEALTHY MIND IN A HEALTHY BODY. WHAT WILL YOU DO TODAY TO STAY ACTIVE?

_____

◼ CONNECTING
WHO WILL YOU TALK TO TODAY TO GET YOU ONE STEP CLOSER TOWARDS REACHING YOUR GOAL?

_____

_____

 EVENING REFLECTION

◼ TODAY'S WINS
NOW THAT THE DAY IS OVER, REFLECT ON WHAT YOU DID TODAY THAT HELPED YOU TO GET CLOSER TO YOUR BIG GOAL

_____   _____

_____   _____

◼ PUSHING BEYOND
WHAT CAN YOU DO TOMORRROW TO IMPROVE ON THE LESSONS THAT YOU LEARNED TODAY?

_____

_____

_____

DAY ____

> " *The only thing standing between you and your goal is the bullshit story you keep telling yourself as to why you can't achieve it.* — *Jordan Belfort*

■ THE BIG GOAL

WHAT WILL YOU ACHIEVE TODAY TO GET YOU ONE STEP CLOSER TO ACHIEVING YOUR DREAM?

_____

_____

■ TAKING ACTION

WHAT STEPS WILL YOU TAKE TODAY TO ENSURE THAT YOU REACH YOUR BIG GOAL?

1 _____

2 _____

3 _____

■ MORNING RITUAL

SUCCESS STARTS IN THE HABITS YOU CREATE FROM THE TIME YOU WAKE UP. HOW WILL YOU PREPARE YOUR MIND FOR ACTION TODAY?

I WILL _____

I WILL _____

I WILL _____

■ GRATITUDE

PEOPLE WHO PRACTICE THE HABIT OF GRATITUDE ATTRACT MORE SUCCESS. WHO OR WHAT ARE YOU GRATEFUL FOR TODAY?

_____   _____

_____   _____

_____   _____

DAY ____

FACEBOOK CHECK-IN

COMMENT ON TODAY'S POST IN THE **RE-INVENT 360 JOURNAL COMMUNITY** FACEBOOK GROUP.

■ FITNESS FOCUS

A HEALTHY MIND IN A HEALTHY BODY. WHAT WILL YOU DO TODAY TO STAY ACTIVE?

_____

■ CONNECTING

WHO WILL YOU TALK TO TODAY TO GET YOU ONE STEP CLOSER TOWARDS REACHING YOUR GOAL?

_____

_____

☽ EVENING REFLECTION

■ TODAY'S WINS

NOW THAT THE DAY IS OVER, REFLECT ON WHAT YOU DID TODAY THAT HELPED YOU TO GET CLOSER TO YOUR BIG GOAL

_____   _____

_____   _____

■ PUSHING BEYOND

WHAT CAN YOU DO TOMORRROW TO IMPROVE ON THE LESSONS THAT YOU LEARNED TODAY?

_____

_____

_____

DAY ____

DATE _____

■ THE BIG GOAL

WHAT WILL YOU ACHIEVE TODAY TO GET YOU ONE STEP CLOSER TO ACHIEVING YOUR DREAM?

_____

_____

■ TAKING ACTION

WHAT STEPS WILL YOU TAKE TODAY TO ENSURE THAT YOU REACH YOUR BIG GOAL?

1 _____

2 _____

3 _____

■ MORNING RITUAL

SUCCESS STARTS IN THE HABITS YOU CREATE FROM THE TIME YOU WAKE UP. HOW WILL YOU PREPARE YOUR MIND FOR ACTION TODAY?

I WILL _____

I WILL _____

I WILL _____

■ GRATITUDE

PEOPLE WHO PRACTICE THE HABIT OF GRATITUDE ATTRACT MORE SUCCESS. WHO OR WHAT ARE YOU GRATEFUL FOR TODAY?

_____   _____

_____   _____

_____   _____

DAY ____

FACEBOOK CHECK-IN
COMMENT ON TODAY'S POST IN THE **RE-INVENT 360 JOURNAL COMMUNITY** FACEBOOK GROUP.

■ FITNESS FOCUS
A HEALTHY MIND IN A HEALTHY BODY. WHAT WILL YOU DO TODAY TO STAY ACTIVE?

_____

■ CONNECTING
WHO WILL YOU TALK TO TODAY TO GET YOU ONE STEP CLOSER TOWARDS REACHING YOUR GOAL?

_____

_____

 **EVENING REFLECTION**

■ TODAY'S WINS
NOW THAT THE DAY IS OVER, REFLECT ON WHAT YOU DID TODAY THAT HELPED YOU TO GET CLOSER TO YOUR BIG GOAL

_____   _____

_____   _____

■ PUSHING BEYOND
WHAT CAN YOU DO TOMORROW TO IMPROVE ON THE LESSONS THAT YOU LEARNED TODAY?

_____

_____

_____

DAY ___

DATE _____

> *Every man is what he is, because of the dominating thoughts which he permits to occupy his mind.*
> — *Napoleon Hill*

■ THE BIG GOAL

WHAT WILL YOU ACHIEVE TODAY TO GET YOU ONE STEP CLOSER TO ACHIEVING YOUR DREAM?

_____

_____

■ TAKING ACTION

WHAT STEPS WILL YOU TAKE TODAY TO ENSURE THAT YOU REACH YOUR BIG GOAL?

1 _____

2 _____

3 _____

■ MORNING RITUAL

SUCCESS STARTS IN THE HABITS YOU CREATE FROM THE TIME YOU WAKE UP. HOW WILL YOU PREPARE YOUR MIND FOR ACTION TODAY?

I WILL _____

I WILL _____

I WILL _____

■ GRATITUDE

PEOPLE WHO PRACTICE THE HABIT OF GRATITUDE ATTRACT MORE SUCCESS. WHO OR WHAT ARE YOU GRATEFUL FOR TODAY?

_____   _____

_____   _____

_____   _____

DAY ____

FACEBOOK CHECK-IN
COMMENT ON TODAY'S POST IN THE **RE-INVENT 360 JOURNAL COMMUNITY** FACEBOOK GROUP.

■ FITNESS FOCUS
A HEALTHY MIND IN A HEALTHY BODY. WHAT WILL YOU DO TODAY TO STAY ACTIVE?

_____

■ CONNECTING
WHO WILL YOU TALK TO TODAY TO GET YOU ONE STEP CLOSER TOWARDS REACHING YOUR GOAL?

_____

_____

EVENING REFLECTION

■ TODAY'S WINS
NOW THAT THE DAY IS OVER, REFLECT ON WHAT YOU DID TODAY THAT HELPED YOU TO GET CLOSER TO YOUR BIG GOAL

_____   _____

_____   _____

■ PUSHING BEYOND
WHAT CAN YOU DO TOMORRROW TO IMPROVE ON THE LESSONS THAT YOU LEARNED TODAY?

_____

_____

_____

DAY ____

> ❝ *I put zero weight into anyone's opinion about me, because I know exactly who I am.* — *Gary Vaynerchuk*

■ THE BIG GOAL

WHAT WILL YOU ACHIEVE TODAY TO GET YOU ONE STEP CLOSER TO ACHIEVING YOUR DREAM?

_____

_____

■ TAKING ACTION

WHAT STEPS WILL YOU TAKE TODAY TO ENSURE THAT YOU REACH YOUR BIG GOAL?

1 _____

2 _____

3 _____

■ MORNING RITUAL

SUCCESS STARTS IN THE HABITS YOU CREATE FROM THE TIME YOU WAKE UP. HOW WILL YOU PREPARE YOUR MIND FOR ACTION TODAY?

I WILL _____

I WILL _____

I WILL _____

■ GRATITUDE

PEOPLE WHO PRACTICE THE HABIT OF GRATITUDE ATTRACT MORE SUCCESS. WHO OR WHAT ARE YOU GRATEFUL FOR TODAY?

_____   _____

_____   _____

_____   _____

179

DAY ____

FACEBOOK CHECK-IN
COMMENT ON TODAY'S POST IN THE **RE-INVENT 360 JOURNAL COMMUNITY** FACEBOOK GROUP.

■ FITNESS FOCUS
A HEALTHY MIND IN A HEALTHY BODY. WHAT WILL YOU DO TODAY TO STAY ACTIVE?

_____

■ CONNECTING
WHO WILL YOU TALK TO TODAY TO GET YOU ONE STEP CLOSER TOWARDS REACHING YOUR GOAL?

_____

_____

EVENING REFLECTION

■ TODAY'S WINS
NOW THAT THE DAY IS OVER, REFLECT ON WHAT YOU DID TODAY THAT HELPED YOU TO GET CLOSER TO YOUR BIG GOAL

_____   _____

_____   _____

■ PUSHING BEYOND
WHAT CAN YOU DO TOMORRROW TO IMPROVE ON THE LESSONS THAT YOU LEARNED TODAY?

_____

_____

_____

DAY ____

> **"** *When obstacles or difficulties arise, the positive thinker takes them as creative opportunities.*
> — *Norman Vincent Peale*

■ THE BIG GOAL

WHAT WILL YOU ACHIEVE TODAY TO GET YOU ONE STEP CLOSER TO ACHIEVING YOUR DREAM?

_____

_____

■ TAKING ACTION

WHAT STEPS WILL YOU TAKE TODAY TO ENSURE THAT YOU REACH YOUR BIG GOAL?

1 _____

2 _____

3 _____

■ MORNING RITUAL

SUCCESS STARTS IN THE HABITS YOU CREATE FROM THE TIME YOU WAKE UP. HOW WILL YOU PREPARE YOUR MIND FOR ACTION TODAY?

I WILL _____

I WILL _____

I WILL _____

■ GRATITUDE

PEOPLE WHO PRACTICE THE HABIT OF GRATITUDE ATTRACT MORE SUCCESS. WHO OR WHAT ARE YOU GRATEFUL FOR TODAY?

_____   _____

_____   _____

_____   _____

DAY _____

FACEBOOK CHECK-IN

COMMENT ON TODAY'S POST IN THE **RE-INVENT 360 JOURNAL COMMUNITY** FACEBOOK GROUP.

■ FITNESS FOCUS

A HEALTHY MIND IN A HEALTHY BODY. WHAT WILL YOU DO TODAY TO STAY ACTIVE?

_____

■ CONNECTING

WHO WILL YOU TALK TO TODAY TO GET YOU ONE STEP CLOSER TOWARDS REACHING YOUR GOAL?

_____

_____

EVENING REFLECTION

■ TODAY'S WINS

NOW THAT THE DAY IS OVER, REFLECT ON WHAT YOU DID TODAY THAT HELPED YOU TO GET CLOSER TO YOUR BIG GOAL

_____   _____

_____   _____

■ PUSHING BEYOND

WHAT CAN YOU DO TOMORRROW TO IMPROVE ON THE LESSONS THAT YOU LEARNED TODAY?

_____

_____

_____

DAY ____

DATE _____

 Respond to every call that excites your spirit. — Rumi

◢ THE BIG GOAL

WHAT WILL YOU ACHIEVE TODAY TO GET YOU ONE STEP CLOSER TO ACHIEVING YOUR DREAM?

_____

_____

TAKING ACTION

WHAT STEPS WILL YOU TAKE TODAY TO ENSURE THAT YOU REACH YOUR BIG GOAL?

_____

_____

_____

MORNING RITUAL

SUCCESS STARTS IN THE HABITS YOU CREATE FROM THE TIME YOU WAKE UP. HOW WILL YOU PREPARE YOUR MIND FOR ACTION TODAY?

I WILL _____

I WILL _____

I WILL _____

◢ GRATITUDE

PEOPLE WHO PRACTICE THE HABIT OF GRATITUDE ATTRACT MORE SUCCESS. WHO OR WHAT ARE YOU GRATEFUL FOR TODAY?

_____   _____

_____   _____

_____   _____

DAY ____

FACEBOOK CHECK-IN
COMMENT ON TODAY'S POST IN THE **RE-INVENT 360 JOURNAL COMMUNITY** FACEBOOK GROUP.

■ FITNESS FOCUS
A HEALTHY MIND IN A HEALTHY BODY. WHAT WILL YOU DO TODAY TO STAY ACTIVE?

_____

■ CONNECTING
WHO WILL YOU TALK TO TODAY TO GET YOU ONE STEP CLOSER TOWARDS REACHING YOUR GOAL?

_____

_____

EVENING REFLECTION

■ TODAY'S WINS
NOW THAT THE DAY IS OVER, REFLECT ON WHAT YOU DID TODAY THAT HELPED YOU TO GET CLOSER TO YOUR BIG GOAL

_____   _____

_____   _____

■ PUSHING BEYOND
WHAT CAN YOU DO TOMORRROW TO IMPROVE ON THE LESSONS THAT YOU LEARNED TODAY?

_____

_____

_____

DAY ____

" *Love all, trust a few, do wrong to none.*
— William Shakespeare

■ THE BIG GOAL

WHAT WILL YOU ACHIEVE TODAY TO GET YOU ONE STEP CLOSER TO
ACHIEVING YOUR DREAM?

_____

_____

■ TAKING ACTION

WHAT STEPS WILL YOU TAKE TODAY TO ENSURE THAT YOU REACH
YOUR BIG GOAL?

1 _____

2 _____

3 _____

■ MORNING RITUAL

SUCCESS STARTS IN THE HABITS YOU CREATE FROM THE TIME YOU
WAKE UP. HOW WILL YOU PREPARE YOUR MIND FOR ACTION TODAY?

I WILL _____

I WILL _____

I WILL _____

■ GRATITUDE

PEOPLE WHO PRACTICE THE HABIT OF GRATITUDE ATTRACT MORE
SUCCESS. WHO OR WHAT ARE YOU GRATEFUL FOR TODAY?

_____   _____

_____   _____

_____   _____

DAY ____

FACEBOOK CHECK-IN
COMMENT ON TODAY'S POST IN THE **RE-INVENT 360 JOURNAL COMMUNITY** FACEBOOK GROUP.

■ FITNESS FOCUS
A HEALTHY MIND IN A HEALTHY BODY. WHAT WILL YOU DO TODAY TO STAY ACTIVE?

_____

■ CONNECTING
WHO WILL YOU TALK TO TODAY TO GET YOU ONE STEP CLOSER TOWARDS REACHING YOUR GOAL?

_____

_____

EVENING REFLECTION

■ TODAY'S WINS
NOW THAT THE DAY IS OVER, REFLECT ON WHAT YOU DID TODAY THAT HELPED YOU TO GET CLOSER TO YOUR BIG GOAL

_____   _____

_____   _____

■ PUSHING BEYOND
WHAT CAN YOU DO TOMORRROW TO IMPROVE ON THE LESSONS THAT YOU LEARNED TODAY?

_____

_____

_____

DAY ____

❝ *We cannot solve our problems with the same thinking we used when we created them. — Albert Einstein*

■ THE BIG GOAL

WHAT WILL YOU ACHIEVE TODAY TO GET YOU ONE STEP CLOSER TO ACHIEVING YOUR DREAM?

_____

_____

■ TAKING ACTION

WHAT STEPS WILL YOU TAKE TODAY TO ENSURE THAT YOU REACH YOUR BIG GOAL?

_____

2 _____

3 _____

■ MORNING RITUAL

SUCCESS STARTS IN THE HABITS YOU CREATE FROM THE TIME YOU WAKE UP. HOW WILL YOU PREPARE YOUR MIND FOR ACTION TODAY?

I WILL _____

I WILL _____

I WILL _____

■ GRATITUDE

PEOPLE WHO PRACTICE THE HABIT OF GRATITUDE ATTRACT MORE SUCCESS. WHO OR WHAT ARE YOU GRATEFUL FOR TODAY?

_____   _____

_____   _____

_____   _____

DAY _____

FACEBOOK CHECK-IN

COMMENT ON TODAY'S POST IN THE **RE-INVENT 360 JOURNAL COMMUNITY** FACEBOOK GROUP.

■ FITNESS FOCUS

A HEALTHY MIND IN A HEALTHY BODY. WHAT WILL YOU DO TODAY TO STAY ACTIVE?

_____

■ CONNECTING

WHO WILL YOU TALK TO TODAY TO GET YOU ONE STEP CLOSER TOWARDS REACHING YOUR GOAL?

_____

_____

EVENING REFLECTION

■ TODAY'S WINS

NOW THAT THE DAY IS OVER, REFLECT ON WHAT YOU DID TODAY THAT HELPED YOU TO GET CLOSER TO YOUR BIG GOAL

_____   _____

_____   _____

■ PUSHING BEYOND

WHAT CAN YOU DO TOMORRROW TO IMPROVE ON THE LESSONS THAT YOU LEARNED TODAY?

_____

_____

_____

DAY ____

DATE _____

 Energy goes where attention goes. — Michael Bernard

■ THE BIG GOAL

WHAT WILL YOU ACHIEVE TODAY TO GET YOU ONE STEP CLOSER TO ACHIEVING YOUR DREAM?

_____

_____

■ TAKING ACTION

WHAT STEPS WILL YOU TAKE TODAY TO ENSURE THAT YOU REACH YOUR BIG GOAL?

_____

_____

_____

■ MORNING RITUAL

SUCCESS STARTS IN THE HABITS YOU CREATE FROM THE TIME YOU WAKE UP. HOW WILL YOU PREPARE YOUR MIND FOR ACTION TODAY?

I WILL _____

I WILL _____

I WILL _____

■ GRATITUDE

PEOPLE WHO PRACTICE THE HABIT OF GRATITUDE ATTRACT MORE SUCCESS. WHO OR WHAT ARE YOU GRATEFUL FOR TODAY?

_____   _____

_____   _____

_____   _____

DAY ____

FACEBOOK CHECK-IN
COMMENT ON TODAY'S POST IN THE **RE-INVENT 360 JOURNAL COMMUNITY** FACEBOOK GROUP.

■ FITNESS FOCUS
A HEALTHY MIND IN A HEALTHY BODY. WHAT WILL YOU DO TODAY TO STAY ACTIVE?

_____

■ CONNECTING
WHO WILL YOU TALK TO TODAY TO GET YOU ONE STEP CLOSER TOWARDS REACHING YOUR GOAL?

_____

_____

EVENING REFLECTION

■ TODAY'S WINS
NOW THAT THE DAY IS OVER, REFLECT ON WHAT YOU DID TODAY THAT HELPED YOU TO GET CLOSER TO YOUR BIG GOAL

_____   _____

_____   _____

■ PUSHING BEYOND
WHAT CAN YOU DO TOMORRROW TO IMPROVE ON THE LESSONS THAT YOU LEARNED TODAY?

_____

_____

_____

10-DAY
CHECK IN

" "

Tune in to the cosmic
power within you.

SHAZ ALIDINA

10-DAY CHECK IN

■ THE BIG GOAL
HOW MUCH CLOSER ARE YOU TO YOUR GOAL?
(1 – NOT MUCH, 5 – MADE AVERAGE PROGRESS, 10 – BIG STEPS)

CIRCLE ONE: 1   2   3   4   5   6   7   8   9   10

HOW HAS YOUR VISION FOR YOUR BIG GOAL EXPANDED THIS WEEK?
_____
_____
_____

■ TAKING ACTION
WHAT ACTIONS DID YOU FEEL GREAT ABOUT THIS WEEK?
_____
_____
_____

■ MORNING RITUAL
HOW MANY DAYS DID YOU PERFORM YOUR MORNING RITUAL?

CIRCLE ONE: 1   2   3   4   5   6   7   8   9   10

WHICH ACTIVITIES SERVED YOU ESPECIALLY WELL?
_____
_____
_____

■ GRATITUDE
WHICH OF YOUR BIG WINS THIS WEEK ARE YOU MOST GRATEFUL FOR?
_____
_____

HOW CAN YOU BUILD ON THIS WIN?
_____
_____

10-DAY CHECK IN

◼ FITNESS

HOW MANY DAYS DID YOU GET ACTIVE DURING THIS CYCLE?

CIRCLE ONE: 1   2   3   4   5   6   7   8   9   10

IF LESS THAN 5, WHAT CHANGES DO YOU NEED TO MAKE TO CREATE TIME FOR YOUR HEALTH?

_____

_____

◼ CONNECTING

HOW MANY CONNECTIONS DID YOU MAKE THIS WEEK?

CIRCLE ONE: 1   2   3   4   5   6   7   8   9   10

WHICH PERSON PROVED TO BE AN INVALUABLE CONNECTION IN GETTING YOU CLOSER TO YOUR BIG GOAL?

_____

WHAT CAN YOU DO TO IN TURN TO BE AN ASSET TO THEM?

_____

_____

◼ MIND DUMP!

SCRIBBLE OUT EVERYTHING THAT'S ON YOUR MIND AS YOU LOOK TOWARDS THE NEXT 10 DAYS. WHAT NEEDS TO BE DONE? WHO NEEDS TO BE CONTACTED? WHAT TOOLS DO YOU NEED? WRITE. DRAW. DOODLE.

READY. SET.
GO!

DAY ____

> **❝** *Compassion becomes real when we recognize our shared humanity. — Pema Chödrön*

■ THE BIG GOAL

WHAT WILL YOU ACHIEVE TODAY TO GET YOU ONE STEP CLOSER TO ACHIEVING YOUR DREAM?

_____

_____

■ TAKING ACTION

WHAT STEPS WILL YOU TAKE TODAY TO ENSURE THAT YOU REACH YOUR BIG GOAL?

1 _____

2 _____

3 _____

■ MORNING RITUAL

SUCCESS STARTS IN THE HABITS YOU CREATE FROM THE TIME YOU WAKE UP. HOW WILL YOU PREPARE YOUR MIND FOR ACTION TODAY?

I WILL _____

I WILL _____

I WILL _____

■ GRATITUDE

PEOPLE WHO PRACTICE THE HABIT OF GRATITUDE ATTRACT MORE SUCCESS. WHO OR WHAT ARE YOU GRATEFUL FOR TODAY?

_____   _____

_____   _____

_____   _____

DAY ____

**FACEBOOK CHECK-IN**
COMMENT ON TODAY'S POST IN THE **RE-INVENT 360 JOURNAL COMMUNITY** FACEBOOK GROUP.

■ FITNESS FOCUS
A HEALTHY MIND IN A HEALTHY BODY. WHAT WILL YOU DO TODAY TO STAY ACTIVE?

_____

■ CONNECTING
WHO WILL YOU TALK TO TODAY TO GET YOU ONE STEP CLOSER TOWARDS REACHING YOUR GOAL?

_____

_____

☽ EVENING REFLECTION

■ TODAY'S WINS
NOW THAT THE DAY IS OVER, REFLECT ON WHAT YOU DID TODAY THAT HELPED YOU TO GET CLOSER TO YOUR BIG GOAL

_____   _____

_____   _____

■ PUSHING BEYOND
WHAT CAN YOU DO TOMORRROW TO IMPROVE ON THE LESSONS THAT YOU LEARNED TODAY?

_____

_____

_____

DAY ____

DATE _____

> *In the process of letting go you will lose many things from the past, but you will find yourself.*
> — Deepak Chopra

■ THE BIG GOAL

WHAT WILL YOU ACHIEVE TODAY TO GET YOU ONE STEP CLOSER TO ACHIEVING YOUR DREAM?

_____

_____

■ TAKING ACTION

WHAT STEPS WILL YOU TAKE TODAY TO ENSURE THAT YOU REACH YOUR BIG GOAL?

_____

2 _____

3 _____

■ MORNING RITUAL

SUCCESS STARTS IN THE HABITS YOU CREATE FROM THE TIME YOU WAKE UP. HOW WILL YOU PREPARE YOUR MIND FOR ACTION TODAY?

I WILL _____

I WILL _____

I WILL _____

■ GRATITUDE

PEOPLE WHO PRACTICE THE HABIT OF GRATITUDE ATTRACT MORE SUCCESS. WHO OR WHAT ARE YOU GRATEFUL FOR TODAY?

_____   _____

_____   _____

_____   _____

DAY ____

FACEBOOK CHECK-IN
COMMENT ON TODAY'S POST IN THE **RE-INVENT 360 JOURNAL COMMUNITY** FACEBOOK GROUP.

■ FITNESS FOCUS

A HEALTHY MIND IN A HEALTHY BODY. WHAT WILL YOU DO TODAY TO STAY ACTIVE?

_____

■ CONNECTING

WHO WILL YOU TALK TO TODAY TO GET YOU ONE STEP CLOSER TOWARDS REACHING YOUR GOAL?

_____

_____

☾ EVENING REFLECTION

■ TODAY'S WINS

NOW THAT THE DAY IS OVER, REFLECT ON WHAT YOU DID TODAY THAT HELPED YOU TO GET CLOSER TO YOUR BIG GOAL

_____   _____

_____   _____

■ PUSHING BEYOND

WHAT CAN YOU DO TOMORRROW TO IMPROVE ON THE LESSONS THAT YOU LEARNED TODAY?

_____

_____

_____

DAY ____

 You either walk inside your story and own it or you stand outside your story and hustle for your worthiness.
— Brené Brown

■ THE BIG GOAL

WHAT WILL YOU ACHIEVE TODAY TO GET YOU ONE STEP CLOSER TO ACHIEVING YOUR DREAM?

_____

_____

■ TAKING ACTION

WHAT STEPS WILL YOU TAKE TODAY TO ENSURE THAT YOU REACH YOUR BIG GOAL?

1 _____

2 _____

3 _____

■ MORNING RITUAL

SUCCESS STARTS IN THE HABITS YOU CREATE FROM THE TIME YOU WAKE UP. HOW WILL YOU PREPARE YOUR MIND FOR ACTION TODAY?

I WILL _____

I WILL _____

I WILL _____

■ GRATITUDE

PEOPLE WHO PRACTICE THE HABIT OF GRATITUDE ATTRACT MORE SUCCESS. WHO OR WHAT ARE YOU GRATEFUL FOR TODAY?

_____ _____

_____ _____

_____ _____

DAY ____

FACEBOOK CHECK-IN
COMMENT ON TODAY'S POST IN THE **RE-INVENT 360 JOURNAL COMMUNITY** FACEBOOK GROUP.

■ FITNESS FOCUS
A HEALTHY MIND IN A HEALTHY BODY. WHAT WILL YOU DO TODAY TO STAY ACTIVE?

_____

■ CONNECTING
WHO WILL YOU TALK TO TODAY TO GET YOU ONE STEP CLOSER TOWARDS REACHING YOUR GOAL?

_____

_____

 EVENING REFLECTION

■ TODAY'S WINS
NOW THAT THE DAY IS OVER, REFLECT ON WHAT YOU DID TODAY THAT HELPED YOU TO GET CLOSER TO YOUR BIG GOAL

_____   _____

_____   _____

■ PUSHING BEYOND
WHAT CAN YOU DO TOMORRROW TO IMPROVE ON THE LESSONS THAT YOU LEARNED TODAY?

_____

_____

_____

DAY ____

> **❝** *Come out of the masses. Stand alone like a lion and live your life according to your own light. — Osho*

■ THE BIG GOAL

WHAT WILL YOU ACHIEVE TODAY TO GET YOU ONE STEP CLOSER TO ACHIEVING YOUR DREAM?

_____

_____

■ TAKING ACTION

WHAT STEPS WILL YOU TAKE TODAY TO ENSURE THAT YOU REACH YOUR BIG GOAL?

1 _____

2 _____

3 _____

■ MORNING RITUAL

SUCCESS STARTS IN THE HABITS YOU CREATE FROM THE TIME YOU WAKE UP. HOW WILL YOU PREPARE YOUR MIND FOR ACTION TODAY?

I WILL _____

I WILL _____

I WILL _____

■ GRATITUDE

PEOPLE WHO PRACTICE THE HABIT OF GRATITUDE ATTRACT MORE SUCCESS. WHO OR WHAT ARE YOU GRATEFUL FOR TODAY?

_____   _____

_____   _____

_____   _____

201

DAY ____

FACEBOOK CHECK-IN
COMMENT ON TODAY'S POST IN THE **RE-INVENT 360 JOURNAL COMMUNITY** FACEBOOK GROUP.

■ FITNESS FOCUS
A HEALTHY MIND IN A HEALTHY BODY. WHAT WILL YOU DO TODAY TO STAY ACTIVE?

_____

■ CONNECTING
WHO WILL YOU TALK TO TODAY TO GET YOU ONE STEP CLOSER TOWARDS REACHING YOUR GOAL?

_____

_____

EVENING REFLECTION

■ TODAY'S WINS
NOW THAT THE DAY IS OVER, REFLECT ON WHAT YOU DID TODAY THAT HELPED YOU TO GET CLOSER TO YOUR BIG GOAL

_____   _____

_____   _____

■ PUSHING BEYOND
WHAT CAN YOU DO TOMORRROW TO IMPROVE ON THE LESSONS THAT YOU LEARNED TODAY?

_____

_____

_____

DAY ____

" *The only difference between a good day and a bad day is your attitude. — Denis Brown*

■ THE BIG GOAL

WHAT WILL YOU ACHIEVE TODAY TO GET YOU ONE STEP CLOSER TO ACHIEVING YOUR DREAM?

_____

_____

■ TAKING ACTION

WHAT STEPS WILL YOU TAKE TODAY TO ENSURE THAT YOU REACH YOUR BIG GOAL?

1 _____

2 _____

3 _____

■ MORNING RITUAL

SUCCESS STARTS IN THE HABITS YOU CREATE FROM THE TIME YOU WAKE UP. HOW WILL YOU PREPARE YOUR MIND FOR ACTION TODAY?

I WILL _____

I WILL _____

I WILL _____

■ GRATITUDE

PEOPLE WHO PRACTICE THE HABIT OF GRATITUDE ATTRACT MORE SUCCESS. WHO OR WHAT ARE YOU GRATEFUL FOR TODAY?

_____   _____

_____   _____

_____   _____

203

DAY ____

FACEBOOK CHECK-IN
COMMENT ON TODAY'S POST IN THE **RE-INVENT 360 JOURNAL COMMUNITY** FACEBOOK GROUP.

■ FITNESS FOCUS
A HEALTHY MIND IN A HEALTHY BODY. WHAT WILL YOU DO TODAY TO STAY ACTIVE?

■ CONNECTING
WHO WILL YOU TALK TO TODAY TO GET YOU ONE STEP CLOSER TOWARDS REACHING YOUR GOAL?

☾ EVENING REFLECTION

■ TODAY'S WINS
NOW THAT THE DAY IS OVER, REFLECT ON WHAT YOU DID TODAY THAT HELPED YOU TO GET CLOSER TO YOUR BIG GOAL

■ PUSHING BEYOND
WHAT CAN YOU DO TOMORROW TO IMPROVE ON THE LESSONS THAT YOU LEARNED TODAY?

DAY ____

> ❝ *I choose to make the rest of my life the best of my life.*
> *— Louise Hay*

■ THE BIG GOAL

WHAT WILL YOU ACHIEVE TODAY TO GET YOU ONE STEP CLOSER TO ACHIEVING YOUR DREAM?

_____

_____

■ TAKING ACTION

WHAT STEPS WILL YOU TAKE TODAY TO ENSURE THAT YOU REACH YOUR BIG GOAL?

1 _____

2 _____

3 _____

■ MORNING RITUAL

SUCCESS STARTS IN THE HABITS YOU CREATE FROM THE TIME YOU WAKE UP. HOW WILL YOU PREPARE YOUR MIND FOR ACTION TODAY?

I WILL _____

I WILL _____

I WILL _____

■ GRATITUDE

PEOPLE WHO PRACTICE THE HABIT OF GRATITUDE ATTRACT MORE SUCCESS. WHO OR WHAT ARE YOU GRATEFUL FOR TODAY?

_____   _____

_____   _____

_____   _____

205

DAY ____

FACEBOOK CHECK-IN
COMMENT ON TODAY'S POST IN THE **RE-INVENT 360 JOURNAL COMMUNITY** FACEBOOK GROUP.

■ FITNESS FOCUS
A HEALTHY MIND IN A HEALTHY BODY. WHAT WILL YOU DO TODAY TO STAY ACTIVE?

■ CONNECTING
WHO WILL YOU TALK TO TODAY TO GET YOU ONE STEP CLOSER TOWARDS REACHING YOUR GOAL?

EVENING REFLECTION

■ TODAY'S WINS
NOW THAT THE DAY IS OVER, REFLECT ON WHAT YOU DID TODAY THAT HELPED YOU TO GET CLOSER TO YOUR BIG GOAL

■ PUSHING BEYOND
WHAT CAN YOU DO TOMORRROW TO IMPROVE ON THE LESSONS THAT YOU LEARNED TODAY?

DAY ____

DATE _____

> ❝ *Be brave. Take risks. Nothing can substitute experience.*
> *— Paulo Coelho*

■ THE BIG GOAL

WHAT WILL YOU ACHIEVE TODAY TO GET YOU ONE STEP CLOSER TO
ACHIEVING YOUR DREAM?

_____

_____

■ TAKING ACTION

WHAT STEPS WILL YOU TAKE TODAY TO ENSURE THAT YOU REACH
YOUR BIG GOAL?

1 _____

2 _____

3 _____

■ MORNING RITUAL

SUCCESS STARTS IN THE HABITS YOU CREATE FROM THE TIME YOU
WAKE UP. HOW WILL YOU PREPARE YOUR MIND FOR ACTION TODAY?

I WILL _____

I WILL _____

I WILL _____

■ GRATITUDE

PEOPLE WHO PRACTICE THE HABIT OF GRATITUDE ATTRACT MORE
SUCCESS. WHO OR WHAT ARE YOU GRATEFUL FOR TODAY?

_____   _____

_____   _____

_____   _____

DAY _____

FACEBOOK CHECK-IN
COMMENT ON TODAY'S POST IN THE **RE-INVENT 360 JOURNAL COMMUNITY** FACEBOOK GROUP.

■ FITNESS FOCUS
A HEALTHY MIND IN A HEALTHY BODY. WHAT WILL YOU DO TODAY TO STAY ACTIVE?

_____

■ CONNECTING
WHO WILL YOU TALK TO TODAY TO GET YOU ONE STEP CLOSER TOWARDS REACHING YOUR GOAL?

_____

_____

■ TODAY'S WINS
NOW THAT THE DAY IS OVER, REFLECT ON WHAT YOU DID TODAY THAT HELPED YOU TO GET CLOSER TO YOUR BIG GOAL

_____   _____

_____   _____

■ PUSHING BEYOND
WHAT CAN YOU DO TOMORRROW TO IMPROVE ON THE LESSONS THAT YOU LEARNED TODAY?

_____

_____

_____

DAY ___

DATE _____

> " *When you focus on the good, the good gets better.*
> — *Abraham Hicks*

■ THE BIG GOAL

WHAT WILL YOU ACHIEVE TODAY TO GET YOU ONE STEP CLOSER TO
ACHIEVING YOUR DREAM?

_____

_____

■ TAKING ACTION

WHAT STEPS WILL YOU TAKE TODAY TO ENSURE THAT YOU REACH
YOUR BIG GOAL?

1 _____

2 _____

3 _____

■ MORNING RITUAL

SUCCESS STARTS IN THE HABITS YOU CREATE FROM THE TIME YOU
WAKE UP. HOW WILL YOU PREPARE YOUR MIND FOR ACTION TODAY?

I WILL _____

I WILL _____

I WILL _____

■ GRATITUDE

PEOPLE WHO PRACTICE THE HABIT OF GRATITUDE ATTRACT MORE
SUCCESS. WHO OR WHAT ARE YOU GRATEFUL FOR TODAY?

_____   _____

_____   _____

_____   _____

209

DAY ____

 ## FACEBOOK CHECK-IN
COMMENT ON TODAY'S POST IN THE **RE-INVENT 360 JOURNAL COMMUNITY** FACEBOOK GROUP.

■ FITNESS FOCUS
A HEALTHY MIND IN A HEALTHY BODY. WHAT WILL YOU DO TODAY TO STAY ACTIVE?

_____

■ CONNECTING
WHO WILL YOU TALK TO TODAY TO GET YOU ONE STEP CLOSER TOWARDS REACHING YOUR GOAL?

_____

_____

 # EVENING REFLECTION

■ TODAY'S WINS
NOW THAT THE DAY IS OVER, REFLECT ON WHAT YOU DID TODAY THAT HELPED YOU TO GET CLOSER TO YOUR BIG GOAL

_____ _____

_____ _____

■ PUSHING BEYOND
WHAT CAN YOU DO TOMORRROW TO IMPROVE ON THE LESSONS THAT YOU LEARNED TODAY?

_____

_____

_____

DAY ____

DATE _____

> ❝ *If you are happy, happiness will come to you because happiness wants to go where happiness is. — Yogi*

■ THE BIG GOAL

WHAT WILL YOU ACHIEVE TODAY TO GET YOU ONE STEP CLOSER TO ACHIEVING YOUR DREAM?

_____

_____

■ TAKING ACTION

WHAT STEPS WILL YOU TAKE TODAY TO ENSURE THAT YOU REACH YOUR BIG GOAL?

1 _____

2 _____

3 _____

■ MORNING RITUAL

SUCCESS STARTS IN THE HABITS YOU CREATE FROM THE TIME YOU WAKE UP. HOW WILL YOU PREPARE YOUR MIND FOR ACTION TODAY?

I WILL _____

I WILL _____

I WILL _____

■ GRATITUDE

PEOPLE WHO PRACTICE THE HABIT OF GRATITUDE ATTRACT MORE SUCCESS. WHO OR WHAT ARE YOU GRATEFUL FOR TODAY?

_____   _____

_____   _____

_____   _____

DAY _____

 ## FACEBOOK CHECK-IN
COMMENT ON TODAY'S POST IN THE **RE-INVENT 360 JOURNAL COMMUNITY** FACEBOOK GROUP.

■ FITNESS FOCUS
A HEALTHY MIND IN A HEALTHY BODY. WHAT WILL YOU DO TODAY TO STAY ACTIVE?

_____

■ CONNECTING
WHO WILL YOU TALK TO TODAY TO GET YOU ONE STEP CLOSER TOWARDS REACHING YOUR GOAL?

_____

_____

EVENING REFLECTION

■ TODAY'S WINS
NOW THAT THE DAY IS OVER, REFLECT ON WHAT YOU DID TODAY THAT HELPED YOU TO GET CLOSER TO YOUR BIG GOAL

_____   _____

_____   _____

■ PUSHING BEYOND
WHAT CAN YOU DO TOMORROW TO IMPROVE ON THE LESSONS THAT YOU LEARNED TODAY?

_____

_____

_____

DAY ____

> ❝ *When you live with an open heart, unexpected, joyful things happen. — Oprah Winfrey*

■ THE BIG GOAL

WHAT WILL YOU ACHIEVE TODAY TO GET YOU ONE STEP CLOSER TO ACHIEVING YOUR DREAM?

_____

_____

■ TAKING ACTION

WHAT STEPS WILL YOU TAKE TODAY TO ENSURE THAT YOU REACH YOUR BIG GOAL?

1 _____

2 _____

3 _____

■ MORNING RITUAL

SUCCESS STARTS IN THE HABITS YOU CREATE FROM THE TIME YOU WAKE UP. HOW WILL YOU PREPARE YOUR MIND FOR ACTION TODAY?

I WILL _____

I WILL _____

I WILL _____

■ GRATITUDE

PEOPLE WHO PRACTICE THE HABIT OF GRATITUDE ATTRACT MORE SUCCESS. WHO OR WHAT ARE YOU GRATEFUL FOR TODAY?

_____   _____

_____   _____

_____   _____

_____   _____

DAY _____

FACEBOOK CHECK-IN
COMMENT ON TODAY'S POST IN THE **RE-INVENT 360 JOURNAL COMMUNITY** FACEBOOK GROUP.

■ FITNESS FOCUS
A HEALTHY MIND IN A HEALTHY BODY. WHAT WILL YOU DO TODAY TO STAY ACTIVE?

_____

■ CONNECTING
WHO WILL YOU TALK TO TODAY TO GET YOU ONE STEP CLOSER TOWARDS REACHING YOUR GOAL?

_____

_____

EVENING REFLECTION

■ TODAY'S WINS
NOW THAT THE DAY IS OVER, REFLECT ON WHAT YOU DID TODAY THAT HELPED YOU TO GET CLOSER TO YOUR BIG GOAL

_____   _____

_____   _____

■ PUSHING BEYOND
WHAT CAN YOU DO TOMORRROW TO IMPROVE ON THE LESSONS THAT YOU LEARNED TODAY?

_____

_____

_____

10-DAY
CHECK IN

" "

In this ocean called life, ride
your own wave and surf.

SHAZ ALIDINA

10-DAY CHECK IN

■ **THE BIG GOAL**
HOW MUCH CLOSER ARE YOU TO YOUR GOAL?
(1 – NOT MUCH, 5 – MADE AVERAGE PROGRESS, 10 – BIG STEPS)

CIRCLE ONE: 1   2   3   4   5   6   7   8   9   10

HOW HAS YOUR VISION FOR YOUR BIG GOAL EXPANDED THIS WEEK?
_____
_____
_____

■ **TAKING ACTION**
WHAT ACTIONS DID YOU FEEL GREAT ABOUT THIS WEEK?
_____
_____
_____

■ **MORNING RITUAL**
HOW MANY DAYS DID YOU PERFORM YOUR MORNING RITUAL?

CIRCLE ONE: 1   2   3   4   5   6   7   8   9   10

WHICH ACTIVITIES SERVED YOU ESPECIALLY WELL?
_____
_____
_____

■ **GRATITUDE**
WHICH OF YOUR BIG WINS THIS WEEK ARE YOU MOST GRATEFUL FOR?
_____
_____

HOW CAN YOU BUILD ON THIS WIN?
_____
_____

10-DAY CHECK IN

■ FITNESS
HOW MANY DAYS DID YOU GET ACTIVE DURING THIS CYCLE?

CIRCLE ONE: 1   2   3   4   5   6   7   8   9   10

IF LESS THAN 5, WHAT CHANGES DO YOU NEED TO MAKE TO CREATE TIME FOR YOUR HEALTH?

_____

_____

■ CONNECTING
HOW MANY CONNECTIONS DID YOU MAKE THIS WEEK?

CIRCLE ONE: 1   2   3   4   5   6   7   8   9   10

WHICH PERSON PROVED TO BE AN INVALUABLE CONNECTION IN GET-TING YOU CLOSER TO YOUR BIG GOAL?

_____

WHAT CAN YOU DO TO IN TURN TO BE AN ASSET TO THEM?

_____

_____

■ MIND DUMP!
SCRIBBLE OUT EVERYTHING THAT'S ON YOUR MIND AS YOU LOOK TO-WARDS THE NEXT 10 DAYS. WHAT NEEDS TO BE DONE? WHO NEEDS TO BE CONTACTED? WHAT TOOLS DO YOU NEED? WRITE. DRAW. DOODLE.

READY. SET.
GO!

DAY ____

> ❝ *In the midst of movement and chaos, keep stillness inside of you.* — *Deepak Chopra*

■ THE BIG GOAL

WHAT WILL YOU ACHIEVE TODAY TO GET YOU ONE STEP CLOSER TO ACHIEVING YOUR DREAM?

_____

_____

■ TAKING ACTION

WHAT STEPS WILL YOU TAKE TODAY TO ENSURE THAT YOU REACH YOUR BIG GOAL?

1 _____

2 _____

3 _____

■ MORNING RITUAL

SUCCESS STARTS IN THE HABITS YOU CREATE FROM THE TIME YOU WAKE UP. HOW WILL YOU PREPARE YOUR MIND FOR ACTION TODAY?

I WILL _____

I WILL _____

I WILL _____

■ GRATITUDE

PEOPLE WHO PRACTICE THE HABIT OF GRATITUDE ATTRACT MORE SUCCESS. WHO OR WHAT ARE YOU GRATEFUL FOR TODAY?

_____   _____

_____   _____

_____   _____

DAY ____

FACEBOOK CHECK-IN
COMMENT ON TODAY'S POST IN THE **RE-INVENT 360 JOURNAL COMMUNITY** FACEBOOK GROUP.

■ FITNESS FOCUS
A HEALTHY MIND IN A HEALTHY BODY. WHAT WILL YOU DO TODAY TO STAY ACTIVE?

■ CONNECTING
WHO WILL YOU TALK TO TODAY TO GET YOU ONE STEP CLOSER TOWARDS REACHING YOUR GOAL?

EVENING REFLECTION

■ TODAY'S WINS
NOW THAT THE DAY IS OVER, REFLECT ON WHAT YOU DID TODAY THAT HELPED YOU TO GET CLOSER TO YOUR BIG GOAL

■ PUSHING BEYOND
WHAT CAN YOU DO TOMORRROW TO IMPROVE ON THE LESSONS THAT YOU LEARNED TODAY?

DAY ____

> ❝ *The world is changed by your example, not by your opinion. — Timothy Ferriss*

■ THE BIG GOAL

WHAT WILL YOU ACHIEVE TODAY TO GET YOU ONE STEP CLOSER TO ACHIEVING YOUR DREAM?

_____

_____

■ TAKING ACTION

WHAT STEPS WILL YOU TAKE TODAY TO ENSURE THAT YOU REACH YOUR BIG GOAL?

1 _____

2 _____

3 _____

■ MORNING RITUAL

SUCCESS STARTS IN THE HABITS YOU CREATE FROM THE TIME YOU WAKE UP. HOW WILL YOU PREPARE YOUR MIND FOR ACTION TODAY?

I WILL _____

I WILL _____

I WILL _____

■ GRATITUDE

PEOPLE WHO PRACTICE THE HABIT OF GRATITUDE ATTRACT MORE SUCCESS. WHO OR WHAT ARE YOU GRATEFUL FOR TODAY?

_____   _____

_____   _____

_____   _____

_____

DAY ____

FACEBOOK CHECK-IN

COMMENT ON TODAY'S POST IN THE **RE-INVENT 360 JOURNAL COMMUNITY** FACEBOOK GROUP.

■ FITNESS FOCUS

A HEALTHY MIND IN A HEALTHY BODY. WHAT WILL YOU DO TODAY TO STAY ACTIVE?

_____

■ CONNECTING

WHO WILL YOU TALK TO TODAY TO GET YOU ONE STEP CLOSER TOWARDS REACHING YOUR GOAL?

_____

_____

EVENING REFLECTION

■ TODAY'S WINS

NOW THAT THE DAY IS OVER, REFLECT ON WHAT YOU DID TODAY THAT HELPED YOU TO GET CLOSER TO YOUR BIG GOAL

_____   _____

_____   _____

■ PUSHING BEYOND

WHAT CAN YOU DO TOMORRROW TO IMPROVE ON THE LESSONS THAT YOU LEARNED TODAY?

_____

_____

_____

DAY ____

> ❝ *Value yourself, love yourself, treat yourself with such love and respect that when others see you they do the same. — John Edward*

■ THE BIG GOAL

WHAT WILL YOU ACHIEVE TODAY TO GET YOU ONE STEP CLOSER TO ACHIEVING YOUR DREAM?

_____

_____

■ TAKING ACTION

WHAT STEPS WILL YOU TAKE TODAY TO ENSURE THAT YOU REACH YOUR BIG GOAL?

1 _____

2 _____

3 _____

■ MORNING RITUAL

SUCCESS STARTS IN THE HABITS YOU CREATE FROM THE TIME YOU WAKE UP. HOW WILL YOU PREPARE YOUR MIND FOR ACTION TODAY?

I WILL _____

I WILL _____

I WILL _____

■ GRATITUDE

PEOPLE WHO PRACTICE THE HABIT OF GRATITUDE ATTRACT MORE SUCCESS. WHO OR WHAT ARE YOU GRATEFUL FOR TODAY?

_____   _____

_____   _____

_____   _____

FACEBOOK CHECK-IN

COMMENT ON TODAY'S POST IN THE **RE-INVENT 360 JOURNAL COMMUNITY** FACEBOOK GROUP.

■ FITNESS FOCUS

A HEALTHY MIND IN A HEALTHY BODY. WHAT WILL YOU DO TODAY TO STAY ACTIVE?

_____

■ CONNECTING

WHO WILL YOU TALK TO TODAY TO GET YOU ONE STEP CLOSER TOWARDS REACHING YOUR GOAL?

_____

_____

EVENING REFLECTION

■ TODAY'S WINS

NOW THAT THE DAY IS OVER, REFLECT ON WHAT YOU DID TODAY THAT HELPED YOU TO GET CLOSER TO YOUR BIG GOAL

_____   _____

_____   _____

■ PUSHING BEYOND

WHAT CAN YOU DO TOMORROW TO IMPROVE ON THE LESSONS THAT YOU LEARNED TODAY?

_____

_____

_____

DAY _____

> ❝ *Do not be satisfied with the stories that come before you.*
> *Unfold your own myth. — Rumi*

■ THE BIG GOAL

WHAT WILL YOU ACHIEVE TODAY TO GET YOU ONE STEP CLOSER TO
ACHIEVING YOUR DREAM?

_____

_____

■ TAKING ACTION

WHAT STEPS WILL YOU TAKE TODAY TO ENSURE THAT YOU REACH
YOUR BIG GOAL?

1 _____

2 _____

3 _____

■ MORNING RITUAL

SUCCESS STARTS IN THE HABITS YOU CREATE FROM THE TIME YOU
WAKE UP. HOW WILL YOU PREPARE YOUR MIND FOR ACTION TODAY?

I WILL _____

I WILL _____

I WILL _____

■ GRATITUDE

PEOPLE WHO PRACTICE THE HABIT OF GRATITUDE ATTRACT MORE
SUCCESS. WHO OR WHAT ARE YOU GRATEFUL FOR TODAY?

_____   _____

_____   _____

_____   _____

FACEBOOK CHECK-IN

COMMENT ON TODAY'S POST IN THE **RE-INVENT 360 JOURNAL COMMUNITY** FACEBOOK GROUP.

■ FITNESS FOCUS

A HEALTHY MIND IN A HEALTHY BODY. WHAT WILL YOU DO TODAY TO STAY ACTIVE?

■ CONNECTING

WHO WILL YOU TALK TO TODAY TO GET YOU ONE STEP CLOSER TOWARDS REACHING YOUR GOAL?

EVENING REFLECTION

■ TODAY'S WINS

NOW THAT THE DAY IS OVER, REFLECT ON WHAT YOU DID TODAY THAT HELPED YOU TO GET CLOSER TO YOUR BIG GOAL

■ PUSHING BEYOND

WHAT CAN YOU DO TOMORRROW TO IMPROVE ON THE LESSONS THAT YOU LEARNED TODAY?

DAY ____

DATE _____

> **"** *Worrying is using your imagination to create something you don't want. — Abraham Hicks*

■ THE BIG GOAL

WHAT WILL YOU ACHIEVE TODAY TO GET YOU ONE STEP CLOSER TO ACHIEVING YOUR DREAM?

_____

_____

■ TAKING ACTION

WHAT STEPS WILL YOU TAKE TODAY TO ENSURE THAT YOU REACH YOUR BIG GOAL?

1 _____

2 _____

3 _____

■ MORNING RITUAL

SUCCESS STARTS IN THE HABITS YOU CREATE FROM THE TIME YOU WAKE UP. HOW WILL YOU PREPARE YOUR MIND FOR ACTION TODAY?

I WILL _____

I WILL _____

I WILL _____

■ GRATITUDE

PEOPLE WHO PRACTICE THE HABIT OF GRATITUDE ATTRACT MORE SUCCESS. WHO OR WHAT ARE YOU GRATEFUL FOR TODAY?

_____   _____

_____   _____

_____   _____

227

DAY ___

FACEBOOK CHECK-IN
COMMENT ON TODAY'S POST IN THE **RE-INVENT 360 JOURNAL COMMUNITY** FACEBOOK GROUP.

■ FITNESS FOCUS
A HEALTHY MIND IN A HEALTHY BODY. WHAT WILL YOU DO TODAY TO STAY ACTIVE?

■ CONNECTING
WHO WILL YOU TALK TO TODAY TO GET YOU ONE STEP CLOSER TOWARDS REACHING YOUR GOAL?

☾ EVENING REFLECTION

■ TODAY'S WINS
NOW THAT THE DAY IS OVER, REFLECT ON WHAT YOU DID TODAY THAT HELPED YOU TO GET CLOSER TO YOUR BIG GOAL

■ PUSHING BEYOND
WHAT CAN YOU DO TOMORROW TO IMPROVE ON THE LESSONS THAT YOU LEARNED TODAY?

DAY ____

❝ *To live is the rarest thing in the world. Most people exist, that is all.* — Oscar Wilde

■ THE BIG GOAL

WHAT WILL YOU ACHIEVE TODAY TO GET YOU ONE STEP CLOSER TO ACHIEVING YOUR DREAM?

_____

_____

■ TAKING ACTION

WHAT STEPS WILL YOU TAKE TODAY TO ENSURE THAT YOU REACH YOUR BIG GOAL?

1 _____

2 _____

3 _____

■ MORNING RITUAL

SUCCESS STARTS IN THE HABITS YOU CREATE FROM THE TIME YOU WAKE UP. HOW WILL YOU PREPARE YOUR MIND FOR ACTION TODAY?

I WILL _____

I WILL _____

I WILL _____

■ GRATITUDE

PEOPLE WHO PRACTICE THE HABIT OF GRATITUDE ATTRACT MORE SUCCESS. WHO OR WHAT ARE YOU GRATEFUL FOR TODAY?

_____   _____

_____   _____

_____   _____

DAY ____

FACEBOOK CHECK-IN
COMMENT ON TODAY'S POST IN THE **RE-INVENT 360 JOURNAL COMMUNITY** FACEBOOK GROUP.

■ FITNESS FOCUS
A HEALTHY MIND IN A HEALTHY BODY. WHAT WILL YOU DO TODAY TO STAY ACTIVE?

_____

■ CONNECTING
WHO WILL YOU TALK TO TODAY TO GET YOU ONE STEP CLOSER TOWARDS REACHING YOUR GOAL?

_____

_____

 EVENING REFLECTION

■ TODAY'S WINS
NOW THAT THE DAY IS OVER, REFLECT ON WHAT YOU DID TODAY THAT HELPED YOU TO GET CLOSER TO YOUR BIG GOAL

_____   _____

_____   _____

■ PUSHING BEYOND
WHAT CAN YOU DO TOMORRROW TO IMPROVE ON THE LESSONS THAT YOU LEARNED TODAY?

_____

_____

_____

DAY ____

DATE _____

> **"** *Either you run your day, or the day runs you.*
> *— Jim Rohn*

■ THE BIG GOAL

WHAT WILL YOU ACHIEVE TODAY TO GET YOU ONE STEP CLOSER TO ACHIEVING YOUR DREAM?

_____

_____

■ TAKING ACTION

WHAT STEPS WILL YOU TAKE TODAY TO ENSURE THAT YOU REACH YOUR BIG GOAL?

1 _____

2 _____

3 _____

■ MORNING RITUAL

SUCCESS STARTS IN THE HABITS YOU CREATE FROM THE TIME YOU WAKE UP. HOW WILL YOU PREPARE YOUR MIND FOR ACTION TODAY?

I WILL _____

I WILL _____

I WILL _____

■ GRATITUDE

PEOPLE WHO PRACTICE THE HABIT OF GRATITUDE ATTRACT MORE SUCCESS. WHO OR WHAT ARE YOU GRATEFUL FOR TODAY?

_____   _____

_____   _____

_____   _____

DAY ___

FACEBOOK CHECK-IN

COMMENT ON TODAY'S POST IN THE **RE-INVENT 360 JOURNAL COMMUNITY** FACEBOOK GROUP.

■ FITNESS FOCUS

A HEALTHY MIND IN A HEALTHY BODY. WHAT WILL YOU DO TODAY TO STAY ACTIVE?

■ CONNECTING

WHO WILL YOU TALK TO TODAY TO GET YOU ONE STEP CLOSER TOWARDS REACHING YOUR GOAL?

EVENING REFLECTION

■ TODAY'S WINS

NOW THAT THE DAY IS OVER, REFLECT ON WHAT YOU DID TODAY THAT HELPED YOU TO GET CLOSER TO YOUR BIG GOAL

■ PUSHING BEYOND

WHAT CAN YOU DO TOMORRROW TO IMPROVE ON THE LESSONS THAT YOU LEARNED TODAY?

DAY ____

> **❝** *If it is important for you, you will find a way. If it isn't, you will find excuse. — Jason de Makis*

■ THE BIG GOAL

WHAT WILL YOU ACHIEVE TODAY TO GET YOU ONE STEP CLOSER TO ACHIEVING YOUR DREAM?

_____

_____

■ TAKING ACTION

WHAT STEPS WILL YOU TAKE TODAY TO ENSURE THAT YOU REACH YOUR BIG GOAL?

1 _____

2 _____

3 _____

■ MORNING RITUAL

SUCCESS STARTS IN THE HABITS YOU CREATE FROM THE TIME YOU WAKE UP. HOW WILL YOU PREPARE YOUR MIND FOR ACTION TODAY?

I WILL _____

I WILL _____

I WILL _____

■ GRATITUDE

PEOPLE WHO PRACTICE THE HABIT OF GRATITUDE ATTRACT MORE SUCCESS. WHO OR WHAT ARE YOU GRATEFUL FOR TODAY?

_____   _____

_____   _____

_____   _____

DAY ____

FACEBOOK CHECK-IN
COMMENT ON TODAY'S POST IN THE **RE-INVENT 360 JOURNAL COMMUNITY** FACEBOOK GROUP.

■ FITNESS FOCUS
A HEALTHY MIND IN A HEALTHY BODY. WHAT WILL YOU DO TODAY TO STAY ACTIVE?

_____

■ CONNECTING
WHO WILL YOU TALK TO TODAY TO GET YOU ONE STEP CLOSER TOWARDS REACHING YOUR GOAL?

_____

_____

EVENING REFLECTION

■ TODAY'S WINS
NOW THAT THE DAY IS OVER, REFLECT ON WHAT YOU DID TODAY THAT HELPED YOU TO GET CLOSER TO YOUR BIG GOAL

_____   _____

_____   _____

■ PUSHING BEYOND
WHAT CAN YOU DO TOMORRROW TO IMPROVE ON THE LESSONS THAT YOU LEARNED TODAY?

_____

_____

_____

DAY ____

> ❝ *You will never be greater than the thoughts that dominate your mind. — Napoleon Hill*

■ THE BIG GOAL

WHAT WILL YOU ACHIEVE TODAY TO GET YOU ONE STEP CLOSER TO ACHIEVING YOUR DREAM?

_____

_____

■ TAKING ACTION

WHAT STEPS WILL YOU TAKE TODAY TO ENSURE THAT YOU REACH YOUR BIG GOAL?

1 _____

2 _____

3 _____

■ MORNING RITUAL

SUCCESS STARTS IN THE HABITS YOU CREATE FROM THE TIME YOU WAKE UP. HOW WILL YOU PREPARE YOUR MIND FOR ACTION TODAY?

I WILL _____

I WILL _____

I WILL _____

■ GRATITUDE

PEOPLE WHO PRACTICE THE HABIT OF GRATITUDE ATTRACT MORE SUCCESS. WHO OR WHAT ARE YOU GRATEFUL FOR TODAY?

_____   _____

_____   _____

_____   _____

DAY ___

f **FACEBOOK CHECK-IN**
COMMENT ON TODAY'S POST IN THE **RE-INVENT 360 JOURNAL COMMUNITY** FACEBOOK GROUP.

■ FITNESS FOCUS
A HEALTHY MIND IN A HEALTHY BODY. WHAT WILL YOU DO TODAY TO STAY ACTIVE?

___

■ CONNECTING
WHO WILL YOU TALK TO TODAY TO GET YOU ONE STEP CLOSER TOWARDS REACHING YOUR GOAL?

___

___

☾ EVENING REFLECTION

■ TODAY'S WINS
NOW THAT THE DAY IS OVER, REFLECT ON WHAT YOU DID TODAY THAT HELPED YOU TO GET CLOSER TO YOUR BIG GOAL

___ ___

___ ___

■ PUSHING BEYOND
WHAT CAN YOU DO TOMORRROW TO IMPROVE ON THE LESSONS THAT YOU LEARNED TODAY?

___

___

___

DAY ____

> **"** *Every master was a beginner. Every pro was an amateur. Every titan began unknown. Stop waiting. Get going. — Robin Sharma*

■ THE BIG GOAL

WHAT WILL YOU ACHIEVE TODAY TO GET YOU ONE STEP CLOSER TO ACHIEVING YOUR DREAM?

_____

_____

■ TAKING ACTION

WHAT STEPS WILL YOU TAKE TODAY TO ENSURE THAT YOU REACH YOUR BIG GOAL?

1 _____

2 _____

3 _____

■ MORNING RITUAL

SUCCESS STARTS IN THE HABITS YOU CREATE FROM THE TIME YOU WAKE UP. HOW WILL YOU PREPARE YOUR MIND FOR ACTION TODAY?

I WILL _____

I WILL _____

I WILL _____

■ GRATITUDE

PEOPLE WHO PRACTICE THE HABIT OF GRATITUDE ATTRACT MORE SUCCESS. WHO OR WHAT ARE YOU GRATEFUL FOR TODAY?

_____   _____

_____   _____

_____   _____

DAY ____

FACEBOOK CHECK-IN
COMMENT ON TODAY'S POST IN THE **RE-INVENT 360 JOURNAL COMMUNITY** FACEBOOK GROUP.

■ FITNESS FOCUS
A HEALTHY MIND IN A HEALTHY BODY. WHAT WILL YOU DO TODAY TO STAY ACTIVE?

_____

■ CONNECTING
WHO WILL YOU TALK TO TODAY TO GET YOU ONE STEP CLOSER TOWARDS REACHING YOUR GOAL?

_____

_____

EVENING REFLECTION

■ TODAY'S WINS
NOW THAT THE DAY IS OVER, REFLECT ON WHAT YOU DID TODAY THAT HELPED YOU TO GET CLOSER TO YOUR BIG GOAL

_____   _____

_____   _____

■ PUSHING BEYOND
WHAT CAN YOU DO TOMORROW TO IMPROVE ON THE LESSONS THAT YOU LEARNED TODAY?

_____

_____

_____

10-DAY
CHECK IN

" "

Every challenge is preparing you
for tomorrow. Flow with grace!

SHAZ ALIDINA

10-DAY CHECK IN

■ THE BIG GOAL
HOW MUCH CLOSER ARE YOU TO YOUR GOAL?
(1 – NOT MUCH, 5 – MADE AVERAGE PROGRESS, 10 – BIG STEPS)

CIRCLE ONE: 1   2   3   4   5   6   7   8   9   10

HOW HAS YOUR VISION FOR YOUR BIG GOAL EXPANDED THIS WEEK?
_____
_____
_____

■ TAKING ACTION
WHAT ACTIONS DID YOU FEEL GREAT ABOUT THIS WEEK?
_____
_____
_____

■ MORNING RITUAL
HOW MANY DAYS DID YOU PERFORM YOUR MORNING RITUAL?

CIRCLE ONE: 1   2   3   4   5   6   7   8   9   10

WHICH ACTIVITIES SERVED YOU ESPECIALLY WELL?
_____
_____
_____

■ GRATITUDE
WHICH OF YOUR BIG WINS THIS WEEK ARE YOU MOST GRATEFUL FOR?
_____
_____

HOW CAN YOU BUILD ON THIS WIN?
_____
_____

10-DAY CHECK IN

▪ FITNESS
HOW MANY DAYS DID YOU GET ACTIVE DURING THIS CYCLE?

CIRCLE ONE: 1 2 3 4 5 6 7 8 9 10

IF LESS THAN 5, WHAT CHANGES DO YOU NEED TO MAKE TO CREATE TIME FOR YOUR HEALTH?

_____

_____

◢ CONNECTING
HOW MANY CONNECTIONS DID YOU MAKE THIS WEEK?

CIRCLE ONE: 1 2 3 4 5 6 7 8 9 10

WHICH PERSON PROVED TO BE AN INVALUABLE CONNECTION IN GETTING YOU CLOSER TO YOUR BIG GOAL?

_____

WHAT CAN YOU DO TO IN TURN TO BE AN ASSET TO THEM?

_____

_____

▌MIND DUMP!
SCRIBBLE OUT EVERYTHING THAT'S ON YOUR MIND AS YOU LOOK TOWARDS THE NEXT 10 DAYS. WHAT NEEDS TO BE DONE? WHO NEEDS TO BE CONTACTED? WHAT TOOLS DO YOU NEED? WRITE. DRAW. DOODLE.

READY. SET.
GO!

DAY ____

❝❝ *Fear kills growth. — Gary Vaynerchuk*

■ THE BIG GOAL

WHAT WILL YOU ACHIEVE TODAY TO GET YOU ONE STEP CLOSER TO ACHIEVING YOUR DREAM?

_____

_____

■ TAKING ACTION

WHAT STEPS WILL YOU TAKE TODAY TO ENSURE THAT YOU REACH YOUR BIG GOAL?

1 _____

2 _____

3 _____

■ MORNING RITUAL

SUCCESS STARTS IN THE HABITS YOU CREATE FROM THE TIME YOU WAKE UP. HOW WILL YOU PREPARE YOUR MIND FOR ACTION TODAY?

I WILL _____

I WILL _____

I WILL _____

■ GRATITUDE

PEOPLE WHO PRACTICE THE HABIT OF GRATITUDE ATTRACT MORE SUCCESS. WHO OR WHAT ARE YOU GRATEFUL FOR TODAY?

_____   _____

_____   _____

_____   _____

243

f FACEBOOK CHECK-IN
COMMENT ON TODAY'S POST IN THE **RE-INVENT 360 JOURNAL COMMUNITY** FACEBOOK GROUP.

■ FITNESS FOCUS
A HEALTHY MIND IN A HEALTHY BODY. WHAT WILL YOU DO TODAY TO STAY ACTIVE?

_____

■ CONNECTING
WHO WILL YOU TALK TO TODAY TO GET YOU ONE STEP CLOSER TOWARDS REACHING YOUR GOAL?

_____

_____

☾ EVENING REFLECTION

■ TODAY'S WINS
NOW THAT THE DAY IS OVER, REFLECT ON WHAT YOU DID TODAY THAT HELPED YOU TO GET CLOSER TO YOUR BIG GOAL

_____   _____

_____   _____

■ PUSHING BEYOND
WHAT CAN YOU DO TOMORRROW TO IMPROVE ON THE LESSONS THAT YOU LEARNED TODAY?

_____

_____

_____

244

DAY ____

> **Find your own truth. What calls to your heart. What moves your spirit. Make your life dance to the song of your own essence. — Unknown**

■ THE BIG GOAL

WHAT WILL YOU ACHIEVE TODAY TO GET YOU ONE STEP CLOSER TO ACHIEVING YOUR DREAM?

_____

_____

■ TAKING ACTION

WHAT STEPS WILL YOU TAKE TODAY TO ENSURE THAT YOU REACH YOUR BIG GOAL?

1 _____

2 _____

3 _____

■ MORNING RITUAL

SUCCESS STARTS IN THE HABITS YOU CREATE FROM THE TIME YOU WAKE UP. HOW WILL YOU PREPARE YOUR MIND FOR ACTION TODAY?

I WILL _____

I WILL _____

I WILL _____

■ GRATITUDE

PEOPLE WHO PRACTICE THE HABIT OF GRATITUDE ATTRACT MORE SUCCESS. WHO OR WHAT ARE YOU GRATEFUL FOR TODAY?

_____   _____

_____   _____

_____   _____

DAY ____

FACEBOOK CHECK-IN

COMMENT ON TODAY'S POST IN THE **RE-INVENT 360 JOURNAL COMMUNITY** FACEBOOK GROUP.

■ FITNESS FOCUS

A HEALTHY MIND IN A HEALTHY BODY. WHAT WILL YOU DO TODAY TO STAY ACTIVE?

■ CONNECTING

WHO WILL YOU TALK TO TODAY TO GET YOU ONE STEP CLOSER TOWARDS REACHING YOUR GOAL?

EVENING REFLECTION

■ TODAY'S WINS

NOW THAT THE DAY IS OVER, REFLECT ON WHAT YOU DID TODAY THAT HELPED YOU TO GET CLOSER TO YOUR BIG GOAL

■ PUSHING BEYOND

WHAT CAN YOU DO TOMORROW TO IMPROVE ON THE LESSONS THAT YOU LEARNED TODAY?

DAY _____

> **"** *It always seems impossible until it's done.*
> *— Nelson Mandela*

■ THE BIG GOAL

WHAT WILL YOU ACHIEVE TODAY TO GET YOU ONE STEP CLOSER TO ACHIEVING YOUR DREAM?

_____

_____

■ TAKING ACTION

WHAT STEPS WILL YOU TAKE TODAY TO ENSURE THAT YOU REACH YOUR BIG GOAL?

1 _____

2 _____

3 _____

■ MORNING RITUAL

SUCCESS STARTS IN THE HABITS YOU CREATE FROM THE TIME YOU WAKE UP. HOW WILL YOU PREPARE YOUR MIND FOR ACTION TODAY?

I WILL _____

I WILL _____

I WILL _____

■ GRATITUDE

PEOPLE WHO PRACTICE THE HABIT OF GRATITUDE ATTRACT MORE SUCCESS. WHO OR WHAT ARE YOU GRATEFUL FOR TODAY?

_____   _____

_____   _____

_____   _____

DAY ____

FACEBOOK CHECK-IN
COMMENT ON TODAY'S POST IN THE **RE-INVENT 360 JOURNAL COMMUNITY** FACEBOOK GROUP.

■ FITNESS FOCUS
A HEALTHY MIND IN A HEALTHY BODY. WHAT WILL YOU DO TODAY TO STAY ACTIVE?

■ CONNECTING
WHO WILL YOU TALK TO TODAY TO GET YOU ONE STEP CLOSER TOWARDS REACHING YOUR GOAL?

EVENING REFLECTION

■ TODAY'S WINS
NOW THAT THE DAY IS OVER, REFLECT ON WHAT YOU DID TODAY THAT HELPED YOU TO GET CLOSER TO YOUR BIG GOAL

■ PUSHING BEYOND
WHAT CAN YOU DO TOMORROW TO IMPROVE ON THE LESSONS THAT YOU LEARNED TODAY?

DAY ____

> " *When you say yes to others, make sure you are not saying no to yourself.* — Paolo Coelho

■ THE BIG GOAL

WHAT WILL YOU ACHIEVE TODAY TO GET YOU ONE STEP CLOSER TO ACHIEVING YOUR DREAM?

_____

_____

■ TAKING ACTION

WHAT STEPS WILL YOU TAKE TODAY TO ENSURE THAT YOU REACH YOUR BIG GOAL?

1 _____

2 _____

3 _____

■ MORNING RITUAL

SUCCESS STARTS IN THE HABITS YOU CREATE FROM THE TIME YOU WAKE UP. HOW WILL YOU PREPARE YOUR MIND FOR ACTION TODAY?

I WILL _____

I WILL _____

I WILL _____

■ GRATITUDE

PEOPLE WHO PRACTICE THE HABIT OF GRATITUDE ATTRACT MORE SUCCESS. WHO OR WHAT ARE YOU GRATEFUL FOR TODAY?

_____   _____

_____   _____

_____   _____

DAY ____

FACEBOOK CHECK-IN
COMMENT ON TODAY'S POST IN THE **RE-INVENT 360 JOURNAL COMMUNITY** FACEBOOK GROUP.

■ FITNESS FOCUS
A HEALTHY MIND IN A HEALTHY BODY. WHAT WILL YOU DO TODAY TO STAY ACTIVE?

_____

■ CONNECTING
WHO WILL YOU TALK TO TODAY TO GET YOU ONE STEP CLOSER TOWARDS REACHING YOUR GOAL?

_____

_____

EVENING REFLECTION

■ TODAY'S WINS
NOW THAT THE DAY IS OVER, REFLECT ON WHAT YOU DID TODAY THAT HELPED YOU TO GET CLOSER TO YOUR BIG GOAL

_____   _____

_____   _____

■ PUSHING BEYOND
WHAT CAN YOU DO TOMORROW TO IMPROVE ON THE LESSONS THAT YOU LEARNED TODAY?

_____

_____

_____

DAY ____

> **“** *People with goals succeed because they know where they are going. — Earl Nightingale*

■ THE BIG GOAL

WHAT WILL YOU ACHIEVE TODAY TO GET YOU ONE STEP CLOSER TO ACHIEVING YOUR DREAM?

_____

_____

■ TAKING ACTION

WHAT STEPS WILL YOU TAKE TODAY TO ENSURE THAT YOU REACH YOUR BIG GOAL?

1 _____

2 _____

3 _____

■ MORNING RITUAL

SUCCESS STARTS IN THE HABITS YOU CREATE FROM THE TIME YOU WAKE UP. HOW WILL YOU PREPARE YOUR MIND FOR ACTION TODAY?

I WILL _____

I WILL _____

I WILL _____

■ GRATITUDE

PEOPLE WHO PRACTICE THE HABIT OF GRATITUDE ATTRACT MORE SUCCESS. WHO OR WHAT ARE YOU GRATEFUL FOR TODAY?

_____   _____

_____   _____

_____   _____

DAY _____

FACEBOOK CHECK-IN
COMMENT ON TODAY'S POST IN THE **RE-INVENT 360 JOURNAL COMMUNITY** FACEBOOK GROUP.

■ FITNESS FOCUS
A HEALTHY MIND IN A HEALTHY BODY. WHAT WILL YOU DO TODAY TO STAY ACTIVE?

_____

■ CONNECTING
WHO WILL YOU TALK TO TODAY TO GET YOU ONE STEP CLOSER TOWARDS REACHING YOUR GOAL?

_____

_____

■ TODAY'S WINS
NOW THAT THE DAY IS OVER, REFLECT ON WHAT YOU DID TODAY THAT HELPED YOU TO GET CLOSER TO YOUR BIG GOAL

_____   _____

_____   _____

■ PUSHING BEYOND
WHAT CAN YOU DO TOMORRROW TO IMPROVE ON THE LESSONS THAT YOU LEARNED TODAY?

_____

_____

_____

ReInvent360Journal.com

DAY ____

> **❝❝** *Stop holding yourself back. If you aren't happy, make a change. — Unknown*

■ THE BIG GOAL

WHAT WILL YOU ACHIEVE TODAY TO GET YOU ONE STEP CLOSER TO ACHIEVING YOUR DREAM?

_____

_____

■ TAKING ACTION

WHAT STEPS WILL YOU TAKE TODAY TO ENSURE THAT YOU REACH YOUR BIG GOAL?

1 _____

2 _____

3 _____

■ MORNING RITUAL

SUCCESS STARTS IN THE HABITS YOU CREATE FROM THE TIME YOU WAKE UP. HOW WILL YOU PREPARE YOUR MIND FOR ACTION TODAY?

I WILL _____

I WILL _____

I WILL _____

■ GRATITUDE

PEOPLE WHO PRACTICE THE HABIT OF GRATITUDE ATTRACT MORE SUCCESS. WHO OR WHAT ARE YOU GRATEFUL FOR TODAY?

_____   _____

_____   _____

_____   _____

FACEBOOK CHECK-IN
COMMENT ON TODAY'S POST IN THE **RE-INVENT 360 JOURNAL COMMUNITY** FACEBOOK GROUP.

■ FITNESS FOCUS
A HEALTHY MIND IN A HEALTHY BODY. WHAT WILL YOU DO TODAY TO STAY ACTIVE?

_____

■ CONNECTING
WHO WILL YOU TALK TO TODAY TO GET YOU ONE STEP CLOSER TOWARDS REACHING YOUR GOAL?

_____

_____

 # EVENING REFLECTION

■ TODAY'S WINS
NOW THAT THE DAY IS OVER, REFLECT ON WHAT YOU DID TODAY THAT HELPED YOU TO GET CLOSER TO YOUR BIG GOAL

_____   _____

_____   _____

■ PUSHING BEYOND
WHAT CAN YOU DO TOMORRROW TO IMPROVE ON THE LESSONS THAT YOU LEARNED TODAY?

_____

_____

_____

DAY ____

DATE _____

> 66 *If you want to change your attitude, change the stories you tell yourself.* — *Jay Shetty*

■ THE BIG GOAL

WHAT WILL YOU ACHIEVE TODAY TO GET YOU ONE STEP CLOSER TO ACHIEVING YOUR DREAM?

_____

_____

■ TAKING ACTION

WHAT STEPS WILL YOU TAKE TODAY TO ENSURE THAT YOU REACH YOUR BIG GOAL?

1 _____

2 _____

3 _____

■ MORNING RITUAL

SUCCESS STARTS IN THE HABITS YOU CREATE FROM THE TIME YOU WAKE UP. HOW WILL YOU PREPARE YOUR MIND FOR ACTION TODAY?

I WILL _____

I WILL _____

I WILL _____

■ GRATITUDE

PEOPLE WHO PRACTICE THE HABIT OF GRATITUDE ATTRACT MORE SUCCESS. WHO OR WHAT ARE YOU GRATEFUL FOR TODAY?

_____   _____

_____   _____

_____   _____

DAY ____

FACEBOOK CHECK-IN

COMMENT ON TODAY'S POST IN THE **RE-INVENT 360 JOURNAL COMMUNITY** FACEBOOK GROUP.

■ FITNESS FOCUS

A HEALTHY MIND IN A HEALTHY BODY. WHAT WILL YOU DO TODAY TO STAY ACTIVE?

_____

■ CONNECTING

WHO WILL YOU TALK TO TODAY TO GET YOU ONE STEP CLOSER TOWARDS REACHING YOUR GOAL?

_____

_____

EVENING REFLECTION

■ TODAY'S WINS

NOW THAT THE DAY IS OVER, REFLECT ON WHAT YOU DID TODAY THAT HELPED YOU TO GET CLOSER TO YOUR BIG GOAL

_____   _____

_____   _____

■ PUSHING BEYOND

WHAT CAN YOU DO TOMORRROW TO IMPROVE ON THE LESSONS THAT YOU LEARNED TODAY?

_____

_____

_____

DAY ____

> **❝** *In the tapestry of life we are all connected. Each one of us is a gift to those around us, helping each other be who we are, weaving a perfect picture together. — Anita Moorjani*

■ THE BIG GOAL

WHAT WILL YOU ACHIEVE TODAY TO GET YOU ONE STEP CLOSER TO ACHIEVING YOUR DREAM?

_____

_____

■ TAKING ACTION

WHAT STEPS WILL YOU TAKE TODAY TO ENSURE THAT YOU REACH YOUR BIG GOAL?

1 _____

2 _____

3 _____

■ MORNING RITUAL

SUCCESS STARTS IN THE HABITS YOU CREATE FROM THE TIME YOU WAKE UP. HOW WILL YOU PREPARE YOUR MIND FOR ACTION TODAY?

I WILL _____

I WILL _____

I WILL _____

■ GRATITUDE

PEOPLE WHO PRACTICE THE HABIT OF GRATITUDE ATTRACT MORE SUCCESS. WHO OR WHAT ARE YOU GRATEFUL FOR TODAY?

_____   _____

_____   _____

_____   _____

DAY ____

FACEBOOK CHECK-IN

COMMENT ON TODAY'S POST IN THE **RE-INVENT 360 JOURNAL COMMUNITY** FACEBOOK GROUP.

■ FITNESS FOCUS

A HEALTHY MIND IN A HEALTHY BODY. WHAT WILL YOU DO TODAY TO STAY ACTIVE?

_____

■ CONNECTING

WHO WILL YOU TALK TO TODAY TO GET YOU ONE STEP CLOSER TOWARDS REACHING YOUR GOAL?

_____

_____

■ TODAY'S WINS

NOW THAT THE DAY IS OVER, REFLECT ON WHAT YOU DID TODAY THAT HELPED YOU TO GET CLOSER TO YOUR BIG GOAL

_____   _____

_____   _____

■ PUSHING BEYOND

WHAT CAN YOU DO TOMORRROW TO IMPROVE ON THE LESSONS THAT YOU LEARNED TODAY?

_____

_____

_____

DAY ____

> **"** *Waste no words on a man who dislikes you. Actions will impress him more. — Napoleon Hill*

■ THE BIG GOAL

WHAT WILL YOU ACHIEVE TODAY TO GET YOU ONE STEP CLOSER TO ACHIEVING YOUR DREAM?

_____

_____

■ TAKING ACTION

WHAT STEPS WILL YOU TAKE TODAY TO ENSURE THAT YOU REACH YOUR BIG GOAL?

1 _____

2 _____

3 _____

■ MORNING RITUAL

SUCCESS STARTS IN THE HABITS YOU CREATE FROM THE TIME YOU WAKE UP. HOW WILL YOU PREPARE YOUR MIND FOR ACTION TODAY?

I WILL _____

I WILL _____

I WILL _____

■ GRATITUDE

PEOPLE WHO PRACTICE THE HABIT OF GRATITUDE ATTRACT MORE SUCCESS. WHO OR WHAT ARE YOU GRATEFUL FOR TODAY?

_____   _____

_____   _____

_____   _____

DAY ____

FACEBOOK CHECK-IN
COMMENT ON TODAY'S POST IN THE **RE-INVENT 360 JOURNAL COMMUNITY** FACEBOOK GROUP.

■ FITNESS FOCUS
A HEALTHY MIND IN A HEALTHY BODY. WHAT WILL YOU DO TODAY TO STAY ACTIVE?

_____

■ CONNECTING
WHO WILL YOU TALK TO TODAY TO GET YOU ONE STEP CLOSER TOWARDS REACHING YOUR GOAL?

_____

_____

EVENING REFLECTION

■ TODAY'S WINS
NOW THAT THE DAY IS OVER, REFLECT ON WHAT YOU DID TODAY THAT HELPED YOU TO GET CLOSER TO YOUR BIG GOAL

_____   _____

_____   _____

■ PUSHING BEYOND
WHAT CAN YOU DO TOMORRROW TO IMPROVE ON THE LESSONS THAT YOU LEARNED TODAY?

_____

_____

_____

DAY ____

> ❝ *The heart is like a garden. It can grow compassion or fear, resentment or love. What seeds will you plant there?*
> *— Buddha*

■ THE BIG GOAL

WHAT WILL YOU ACHIEVE TODAY TO GET YOU ONE STEP CLOSER TO ACHIEVING YOUR DREAM?

_____

_____

■ TAKING ACTION

WHAT STEPS WILL YOU TAKE TODAY TO ENSURE THAT YOU REACH YOUR BIG GOAL?

1 _____

2 _____

3 _____

■ MORNING RITUAL

SUCCESS STARTS IN THE HABITS YOU CREATE FROM THE TIME YOU WAKE UP. HOW WILL YOU PREPARE YOUR MIND FOR ACTION TODAY?

I WILL _____

I WILL _____

I WILL _____

■ GRATITUDE

PEOPLE WHO PRACTICE THE HABIT OF GRATITUDE ATTRACT MORE SUCCESS. WHO OR WHAT ARE YOU GRATEFUL FOR TODAY?

_____ _____

_____ _____

_____ _____

261

DAY _____

FACEBOOK CHECK-IN
COMMENT ON TODAY'S POST IN THE **RE-INVENT 360 JOURNAL COMMUNITY** FACEBOOK GROUP.

■ FITNESS FOCUS
A HEALTHY MIND IN A HEALTHY BODY. WHAT WILL YOU DO TODAY TO STAY ACTIVE?

_____

■ CONNECTING
WHO WILL YOU TALK TO TODAY TO GET YOU ONE STEP CLOSER TOWARDS REACHING YOUR GOAL?

_____

_____

■ TODAY'S WINS
NOW THAT THE DAY IS OVER, REFLECT ON WHAT YOU DID TODAY THAT HELPED YOU TO GET CLOSER TO YOUR BIG GOAL

_____   _____

_____   _____

■ PUSHING BEYOND
WHAT CAN YOU DO TOMORRROW TO IMPROVE ON THE LESSONS THAT YOU LEARNED TODAY?

_____

_____

_____

10-DAY
CHECK IN

" "

Become addicted to enhancing yourself!

SHAZ ALIDINA

10-DAY CHECK IN

■ THE BIG GOAL
HOW MUCH CLOSER ARE YOU TO YOUR GOAL?
(1 – NOT MUCH, 5 – MADE AVERAGE PROGRESS, 10 – BIG STEPS)

CIRCLE ONE: 1   2   3   4   5   6   7   8   9   10

HOW HAS YOUR VISION FOR YOUR BIG GOAL EXPANDED THIS WEEK?
_____
_____
_____

■ TAKING ACTION
WHAT ACTIONS DID YOU FEEL GREAT ABOUT THIS WEEK?
_____
_____
_____

■ MORNING RITUAL
HOW MANY DAYS DID YOU PERFORM YOUR MORNING RITUAL?

CIRCLE ONE: 1   2   3   4   5   6   7   8   9   10

WHICH ACTIVITIES SERVED YOU ESPECIALLY WELL?
_____
_____
_____

■ GRATITUDE
WHICH OF YOUR BIG WINS THIS WEEK ARE YOU MOST GRATEFUL FOR?
_____
_____

HOW CAN YOU BUILD ON THIS WIN?
_____
_____

10-DAY CHECK IN

■ FITNESS

HOW MANY DAYS DID YOU GET ACTIVE DURING THIS CYCLE?

CIRCLE ONE: 1   2   3   4   5   6   7   8   9   10

IF LESS THAN 5, WHAT CHANGES DO YOU NEED TO MAKE TO CREATE TIME FOR YOUR HEALTH?

_____

_____

■ CONNECTING

HOW MANY CONNECTIONS DID YOU MAKE THIS WEEK?

CIRCLE ONE: 1   2   3   4   5   6   7   8   9   10

WHICH PERSON PROVED TO BE AN INVALUABLE CONNECTION IN GETTING YOU CLOSER TO YOUR BIG GOAL?

_____

WHAT CAN YOU DO TO IN TURN TO BE AN ASSET TO THEM?

_____

_____

■ MIND DUMP!

SCRIBBLE OUT EVERYTHING THAT'S ON YOUR MIND AS YOU LOOK TOWARDS THE NEXT 10 DAYS. WHAT NEEDS TO BE DONE? WHO NEEDS TO BE CONTACTED? WHAT TOOLS DO YOU NEED? WRITE. DRAW. DOODLE.

ELITE COACHING WITH SHAZ ALIDINA

ONE-ON-ONE COACHING

Reclaim Your Life Back!

Transform your mind and start living a more full and meaningful life. It doesn't matter where you are in life, these 3 months will teach you how to overcome limitations, gain clarity, help you create lasting changes and take persistent action towards your goals and dreams.

Get Started: Are you ready to step up, rise above and take action? Visit www. ShazAlidina.com

ELITE COACHING

Stay at the Top of Your Game!

Shaz works with a select number of elite clients. Those who choose Shaz want balanced, vibrant, and energizing life that supports, inspires and magnifies their dreams

Each of us is equipped with the most powerful tool imaginable. There is a famous quote that states, "Whatever the mind can conceive and believe, the mind can achieve." Thus, Shaz coaches, empowers and drives high achieving professionals, such as business leaders, professional athletes, celebrities, singers, designers, ambassadors, and government officials in using this powerful tool to shine with the light of their own divinity.

Every elite needs a professional coach and motivator whose expertise will help achieve your vision and keep you at the top of your game where you'll thrive, and not just survive. Shaz can boost your confidence, help you overcome fears and setbacks, and move you towards advancement. She can help you reclaim your Inner self! and help you to be balanced, vibrant, and energised in a way that supports, inspires, and magnifies your dreams.

Get Started: Are you ready to set up, rise above and take action? Visit www. ShazAlidina.com

FACEBOOK COMMUNITY

Re-Invent 360

Join Shaz and other life changers in the free Facebook group, The Re-Invent 360 Journal Community! Visit www.ReInvent360Journal.com/community to join today!

ABOUT SHAZ ALIDINA

Shaz Alidina is an internationally-certified life coach who elevates high achievers, influencers, and celebrities toward their greatest level of thriving and inner peace. Based in Dubai, Shaz has built a coaching business that spans the globe and is comprised of people and groups in every station in life from enterprising women and home makers to celebrities and leaders. Those she coaches possess the same goal—to achieve more success, to become balanced and to find fulfillment in life. Beginning with self mastery, Shaz teaches her clients how to unlock the limitless possibilities inherently found within.

Born in Africa and surrounded by nature's vibrant colors and creations, it made her fall in love with herself and the energy that created her. Her growth towards self-development and believing in the giant within her made her to continually seek for more. She believes that for miracles to happen, one has to nurture and nourish the within in order to create a flow on the outside, Inside-Out Reality. Her well established career in Interior Designing was not enough to make her heart sing. Through her highs and lows in life she began her quest for true empowerment and today her heart sings with joy every time she touches someone's life through her Life Coaching skills and compassionate nature.

In addition to her coaching, Shaz has spent the last decade furthering her knowledge and skills under great minds such as the internationally bestselling authors Tony Robbins, Louise Hay, Wayne Dyer, Abraham Hicks, Sadhguru, Deepak Chopra and Robin Sharma to name a few, all of whom have transformed the lives of millions through their books, seminars and personal coaching. Shaz is Celebrity Life Coach who has coached and transformed many peoples lives globally with her skills as a Master Life Coach, NLP Master Practitioner, Master Hypnotist, Time-Line Therapy Master Practitioner, Relationship Coach and psychotherapist.

NOTES

NOTES

NOTES